Acclaim for
Relationship Transformation

*"Too often people seek couples therapy in hopes their partners will
change—usually a lost cause. I love the ways the stories and exercises
invite you to first explore your own style of thinking and communication
so you can transform your conversations from trying to prove yourself
right to seeking genuine intimacy. Although designed as a self-study
book for couples, it applies to all types of relationships, and could
help those who are single to prepare for a healthy relationship."*

—Cynthia L. Wall, LCSW, author of *The Courage to Trust:
a guide to building deep and lasting relationships*

Relationship
Transformation

{HAVE YOUR CAKE AND EAT IT TOO}

A Practical Guide for Couples Who
Want to Be Free and Connected

Jerry Duberstein, PhD
and
Mary Ellen Goggin, JD

RELATIONSHIP TRANSFORMATION
Have Your Cake And Eat it Too
© 2012 Jerry Duberstein, Ph.D. and Mary Ellen Goggin, J.D.

Ryder Ridge Press
P.O. Box 1770
Mendocino, California 95460
707-412-8801

www.freeandconnected.com

Cover design by Lori Paquette
www.flirtygirl.com
Book design by Cypress House

PUBLISHER'S CATALOGING-IN-PUBLICATION DATA

Duberstein, Jerry.
    Relationship transformation-- have your cake and eat it too : a practical guide for couples who want to be free and connected / by Jerry Duberstein and Mary Ellen Goggin. -- 1st ed. -- Mendocino, CA : Ryder Ridge Press, c2012.
    p. ; cm.

    ISBN: 978-0-9854177-0-3
    1. Couples--Psychology. 2. Marriage--Psychological aspects.
3. Man-woman relationships--Psychological aspects. 4. Men--Identity. 5. Women--Identity. I. Goggin, Mary Ellen. II. Title.
    HQ801 .D83 2012   2012905667
    646.7/82--dc23 1207

PRINTED IN THE USA
2 4 6 8 9 7 5 3
First edition

Dedication

*To all who yearn for both freedom
and commitment in their relationship.
May you have your cake and eat it too.*

Contents

Preface

I wrote this book with my wife, Mary Ellen Goggin. Designating her as a second writer doesn't do justice to all of her work and the variety of roles she played in getting this book to print. Mary Ellen is a co-creator and was integral at each stage of development. For the past four years we have lived and toiled together to write *Relationship Transformation: Have Your Cake and Eat It Too* and make the book a reality. Mary Ellen's imprint is on every page. Without her brainpower, ideas, and effort, this book would not exist.

For my part, I am the therapist who worked with the couples discussed in the case studies. It is through my eyes and perceptions that the situations are recalled and recounted. I'm the one responsible for the theoretical framework of the process we describe in the book. My earlier inclination was to write a book for couples therapists, loaded with the lingo psychologists love to bandy about with one another. Mary Ellen's sensibilities in shaping the final product helped make this book accessible to everyone. She has a keen awareness of how to get the message across to everyday couples who want better relationships.

This book uses illustrative examples collected during many sessions I spent with my clients over a four-decade career.

Though the substance of these case studies is true, I've disguised my clients' identities by changing names and particular details. The same has been done for friends. The dialog in quotation marks is the essence of what I recall, and not the clients' exact words. The case studies are intended to be didactic — to teach by illustrating themes in methodology. To accomplish this, in some instances, a couple's story is a composite used to demonstrate a specific point. I have tried to be non-offensive in my selection of case studies, and I apologize in advance if the examples used do not represent the full spectrum of today's society.

While I've done my utmost to be gender neutral, I recognize that, having lived my life as a man, certain limitations are inescapable. Mary Ellen provided vital input from a woman's perspective, and shed much-needed wattage on my blind spots. Any lack of gender neutrality in these pages is unintentional.

Jerry Duberstein
2012

Acknowledgments

To all the individuals and couples who shared their stories, for their openness and courage to unearth and speak up for their deepest needs and desires.

To the many writers, scholars, and therapists who helped shape and refine our thinking.

To John Bowlby for his theory of relationship attachment; to Irvin Yalom for redefining existential psychotherapy; and to Steven Mitchell for his exploration of love and freedom in the context of relationship.

To Jan L. Waldron for her faith and friendship.

To the talented writers of the Portsmouth, New Hampshire, writing group for their kindness and perceptive comments.

To Cynthia Frank for her guidance and expertise in the world of publishing and book creation.

To Lori Paquette for the cover design.

To Joe Shaw for his editorial contributions.

To our children whose presence reminds us that with love all things are possible.

Introduction

This book was inspired by all the couples I've spent time with as a therapist over the past forty years. I have been touched by their honesty, courage, and perseverance in saving relationships on the brink of dissolution. These couples wanted more than just an okay relationship; they wanted to experience satisfying love lives. An inner voice nudged them and told them not to give up—there was something better out there.

To have one's cake and eat it too is a popular Old English proverb first recorded in 1546. Its meaning is similar to the phrases "you can't have it both ways" and "you can't have the best of both worlds. The proverb suggests that we reign in our audacious desire to have or want more than we deserve. It speaks of the impossibility of possessing two incompatible things, like oil and water, rain and shine, and darkness and light.

In this book, cake is a metaphor for an exuberant love relationship in which freedom and commitment can coexist. Cake is about joy, sweetness, and levity, the stuff of robust relationships. We celebrate special occasions—birthdays, anniversaries, and weddings—by eating cake together. We love cake—red velvet, orange-glow chiffon, chocolate-raspberry ganache, devil's food, angel food, and strawberry shortcake—to name a few favorites.

Even thinking about cake spreads joy down to the cellular level of our being. Eating cake makes us happy.

Nowadays most people aspire to having the best of all worlds and believe they can achieve it. We, post-moderns sit poised to break through our narrow definitions of relationship and commitment. Deep down we yearn for a committed relationship that gives us enough space to feel free and enough security to feel safe and loved.

We have been given a dualistic relationship model — caged or free, single or saddled, take it or leave it. These outmoded models don't fit our contemporary lifestyles, yet couples get stuck in them by default. People — Millennials, Gen Xers, and Boomers — want more options. They long to loosen the constraints of old models and create relationships that are more congruent with their values and lives.

Our premise — you can have your cake and eat it too — embraces the sacredness of the contemporary values of individual freedom, personal control, and self-realization. To the greatest extent possible, we 21st-century people want a life that allows us to do what we want, when we want, on our own terms. We want a relationship that gives us room to focus on ourselves, and liberates us from feeling solely responsible for our partner's happiness.

We live in an exciting time, a period in which personal growth and transformation are highly valued. Our collective impulse toward freedom is strong. Yet deep connection, forging an enduring bond with another human being, exerts its own gravitational pull. Love has the potential to be one of the most meaningful and satisfying experiences in a lifetime. Freedom without love can be empty.

To lead the exuberant lives we envision, we must embrace a new view of relationships. Each of us is responsible for having the relationship we want. To get it, we need to summon the courage to unearth and speak up for our deepest needs. We can benefit from a newly clarified perspective of our authentic selves and a fresh vision of our ideal relationship. *Relationship Transformation* guides you on a journey to your *cake*.

Times Are Changing

Beginning on the day you were born, your family and culture began to influence you. As a child you observed your parents' interactions, and your experience of them formed the foundation of your beliefs. It continues to influence how you act in relationships even today.

Hollywood stories and Madison Avenue marketing bombarded you with a steady stream of romantic myths. Like most people, you were likely captivated by tales of white knights capturing the hearts of fair maidens, and by examples of infatuated couples who sailed off into the sunset.

Popular culture perpetuates such myths and mistaken beliefs: Your prince will save you, and your partner will always make you happy. If you encounter problems on love's path, it must mean that yours is not really true love after all. To further complicate matters, the structures of traditional marriage roles and expectations have changed and continue to do so, making us long for terra firma as the ground shifts beneath our feet.

Latest statistics reveal that 50 percent of all first marriages end in divorce. These odds increase in second and third marriages. Not included in these numbers are breakups of long-term committed relationships, civil unions, cohabitating couples, and other, similar, unreported private arrangements.

What is particularly troubling about these statistics? They mean that in our mobile 21st-century lifestyles, in which a love relationship is the central connection in people's lives, fewer of us have a chance at developing one. Fewer people live in the community where they were born, or near parents or childhood friends. More people work longer hours, commute farther, or work in isolation at home. Everyone appears to have less opportunity and less time available to build those all-important close ties with others.

In some ways, partners are now more dependent on each other, and expect things normally provided by various other members in a home "village." It's often too much for one person to deliver nurturance, friendship, sustenance, stability, and intellectual stimulation, and be a playmate, confidante, erotic partner, and more.

All these changes impact the nature of our relationships, yet old adages, rules, and expectations persist alongside a new, freedom-oriented zeitgeist, offering weak guidance for today's couples. Based on the latest research and cutting-edge practices, and tempered by good-old common sense, *Relationship Transformation* empowers you to build a relationship suitable for the 21st century.

How This Book Works for You

Relationship Transformation is a book for everyone who wants a happy, enduring relationship. It is a practical guide for couples who yearn for both freedom and commitment in their relationship. We invite you to learn a better way of thinking and relating to yourself and your partner. We share the stories of couples who benefited from our approach and overcame their individual obstacles to love. You get front-row access to their interior lives — their plans and struggles, their conflicting emotions and desires, and their courage to work things out.

One of the couples you'll meet is Anna and Greg, who deal with infidelity and the loss of vitality in their relationship. Can they get past the power imbalance and heal the loss of trust?

When a partner gets tired of an outmoded role and wants

to change the dynamic, it puts strain on the relationship. Bella no longer wants to mother Ed, which makes Ed feel rejected and unloved.

You'll also meet Glenda and Charlene, upended by turmoil over their role reversal. Charlene doesn't want to be the sole breadwinner, and Glenda remains stuck in anger and hurt pride over a career setback.

Eva and Jack, another couple, struggle over individual freedom. On Saturday nights Eva wants to go dancing with her Salsa club. Jack watches hockey games, and expects Eva to be there on the couch beside him. What beliefs and habits need to be uncovered before these couples can solve their problems? Can freedom and connection co-exist in their relationship?

The couples who share their stories vary in age, socioeconomic status, education, career, and ethnicity, yet they have one thing in common: the desire for more robust, satisfying relationships to last a lifetime.

In each case, the couple faces a complicated situation. They resolve issues by looking inside themselves, by being honest, and by trusting and having faith in their connection. Their heartwarming success in solving their problems inspired me to write this book. I wanted more couples to benefit from the Transforming Relationship process by sharing with a wider audience. And from a global perspective, I could make a contribution one couple at a time. Happier couples create a happier, more peaceful world.

Part 1 focuses on transforming your relationship with yourself. You begin by shifting the focus to you rather than concentrating on your partner or the relationship. You'll learn to link your conscious mind with your deepest self, that part of you that knows what's best for you. You will explore the interplay of freedom and secure connection in relationships, and pinpoint the right balance for you. As you learn about your *Inner*

Relationship Fingerprint™, you will get more clarity about yourself and unblock what holds you back. By the end of part 1, you'll know yourself in a different way. You will have identified and articulated what you need and want. Overall, you'll be more confident about getting what you want in your relationship. You'll emerge a more whole♥ person with a greater capacity for connection, and know how to inject the power of *you* into the relationship.

In part 2 you will reconnect with your partner, reinvigorated and with a fresh sense of purpose. With guidance, you and your partner (who we hope takes this journey with you) will build a strong and lasting foundation and create a compelling shared vision that honors your individual uniqueness. Two whole people will link to form a robust, strong, and lasting "us." Finally, you'll have the opportunity to negotiate an agreement to support your vision.

Relationship Transformation is a system with an individual approach. Step by step, you tune in and connect with yourself and then with your partner. No one kind of relationship is offered as a panacea; rather, you get to create the one that works for you. Your path through this book is action-oriented. Time-tested tools, exercises, quizzes, and surveys will help get you where you want to go. You and your partner can use these tools at different stages of your lives. To preserve these pages for multiple uses and users, we suggest that you photocopy the exercises, write your answers only on the photocopies, and save your filled-in pages in a binder—thus creating a personal journal of the process. Alternatively, all of these tools can be downloaded at www.freeandconnected.com. You can print them and create your personal journal from the printed pages.

♥ A "whole" person is fully functional emotionally, psychologically, and spiritually. A whole person experiences a full spectrum of feelings and is able to be intentional in his or her actions and to be authentic in relationships.

How Is This Book Different from Traditional Relationship Books?

In traditional books and therapy, a diagnosis is made of what ails the relationship, and a treatment plan for its "cure" is designed. Couples learn conflict resolution, anger management, communication skills, and the art of compromise. Often they are encouraged to mold themselves into a specific, one-size-fits-all relationship model.

Yet studies reveal that couples therapy works only 35% of the time. On average, couples live in a troubled relationship for six years before seeking help. By then, negative patterns and the buildup of rage and resentment can make transformation very difficult. In therapy, couples promise to change their behavior without addressing the critical underlying issues that cause their distress. With each compromise a partner makes, he or she becomes more distant from his or her authentic dreams and desires. Partners who compromise too much risk losing themselves in the process.

This book takes a different tack by getting to the root of the problem. *Relationship Transformation* will change the way you think about your relationship. First you connect with your deepest self and get access to your desires and dreams. With the help of targeted tools you will puncture cultural myths, dissolve distortions, and discard old baggage. By uncovering old patterns and limiting beliefs, you will learn about what holds you back. Then you will collaborate with your partner to create a new vision. *Relationship Transformation* offers a method that puts you in charge. You will build a solid and dynamic relationship to last a lifetime.

Chapter 1

Have Your Cake
And Eat It Too

At our coastal community's annual Fourth of July salmon barbecue, I chatted with a young teacher about the woes of the school system, upcoming elections, and the like. To be polite she asked me about my work. I told her I was writing a book to help couples transform their lives together. I talked about this chapter, since I had worked on it that morning. I described how couples teeter on a tightrope with freedom and commitment on either end, and how tricky it can be to balance these needs, especially for couples who want a dynamic union.

Overhearing the conversation, people drifted over to join us. A retired banker commented a bit heatedly, "I don't buy it. Why get married if freedom is what you're after? Don't get me wrong, it would be great, but marriage and freedom are mutually exclusive."

The teacher shared, "When I was single I felt free as a bird, and it was great, but it got lonely. Now my wings are clipped, and my adventurous side is pretty dormant, like I don't do wilderness hiking or travel, but for now the settled, domestic life works okay. I love my kids and I'm never lonely anymore. Most days the tradeoff is worth it."

A woman in her late seventies yelled from her chaise lounge a distance away, "I've never wanted to get married. Not that I wasn't asked. I like solitude and can't imagine marching to someone else's drumbeat. I've led an exciting life packed with adventure, and rely on friends for my support system."

A woman artist graying at her temples chimed in, "Life is funny. I've been married three times. When I'm married, life turns dull, but when I'm single, although life is more exciting, I miss constant companionship and get lonely. Guess I'm destined for discontentment."

A middle-aged man, tattooed, and with a bandana covering his hair, came over. "Well, I'm a musician. Been playin' guitar my whole life. Had my own band till my early forties when my wife threatened to leave if I spent one more night away doing gigs. So I quit to save my marriage. Now I'm desperately unhappy, maybe even depressed."

"Free, what is free? I choose to go to work, support my family, and do the right thing. Nobody's twisting my arm. Choice—that's my idea of freedom," piped in the owner of a local construction company.

The discussion grew in intensity, and continued until the sun dropped behind the redwoods. The topic had struck a resonant chord. Ideas expressed fit roughly into two camps: the security-minded who choose stable connection over excitement; and the freedom seekers who value excitement over secure connection. Both groups end up disappointed. People don't thrive in either extreme, yet even so they cling to their beliefs. In which camp do you belong?

People ask me if this book offers a solution. Beneath the question lies a glimmer of hope for more vitality in those who've traded freedom for the security of commitment, and for more security in those who value freedom. The real questions to be explored in this chapter are: Can we have both freedom and the security of commitment in the same relationship? If so, how do we structure such a relationship?

Exercise: Do You Know Your Freedom-Security Needs Quotient?

The next exercise will help you identify your freedom and security needs. Be honest. Choose the response that first occurs to you. It's usually the most accurate. No response is more "correct" than any other. Place an "X" on the response that most closely fits you.

	COLUMN A	COLUMN B
1	*I prefer to travel alone.*	*I prefer not to travel alone.*
2	*I like to make my own financial decisions.*	*I like for my partner to make my financial decisions for me.*
3	*When I'm at home, I am most relaxed by myself.*	*When I'm at home, I prefer to have company.*
4	*I find family obligations burdensome.*	*I find family obligations rewarding.*
5	*I dislike having to tell my partner where I'm going.*	*I like my partner to know where I am.*
6	*I am happier when I am not in a relationship.*	*I am happier in relationship.*
7	*I like to think of myself as not being like everyone else.*	*I like to fit in and belong.*
8	*I like going to parties by myself.*	*I don't like going to parties alone.*

COLUMN A	COLUMN B
9	*Being alone is preferable to being with someone just for his or her company.*	*Sometimes I hang out with people just because I don't feel like being by myself.*
10	*I don't like when someone tells me how I feel.*	*I like when my partner helps me to express my feelings.*
11	*In conflict it's important for me to have my way.*	*In conflict peace is more important than having my own way.*
12	*I like to make purchases without a discussion.*	*I prefer help making purchases.*
13	*I am not willing to be in a relationship just for sex.*	*I am willing to be in a relationship just for sex.*
14	*Following rules is difficult for me.*	*Rules are meant to be followed.*
15	*I don't like anyone to tell me how to spend my time.*	*I like to have help scheduling my time.*
16	*I need to control the TV remote.*	*I like someone else to change the channels.*
17	*I like sleeping alone.*	*I like sleeping with someone.*
18	*It annoys me to talk when I don't feel like it.*	*I really enjoy having someone around to talk to.*
19	*I don't want to live up to the expectations of others.*	*My partner's expectations help me achieve goals.*
20	*I fear getting trapped in a relationship.*	*I feel safest when in relationship.*

Scoring: To tally your results, count the number of responses in column A. Give yourself one point for each.

1–8 points: *Your needs revolve around security and stable connection*

9–14 points: *Your needs for security and freedom are mixed.*

15–20 points: *Your needs revolve around freedom.*

Freedom Comes in All Shapes and Sizes

What follows is an overview of the various kinds of freedom and the big challenges they present for couples. As you read, consider how you deal with personal freedom in your relationship.

Freedom to live the life you want: Everyone has different appetites for risk and adventure, and varying needs for security and stable connection. Consciously choosing a lifestyle that balances these competing needs in a way that satisfies both partners can be challenging for couples.

Freedom to be your authentic self: Beginning at birth, we're bombarded by messages telling us who we should be. We're pressured to be more beautiful, funnier, smarter, wiser, richer, kinder, skinnier, sharper, hipper, without regard for who we really are, our authentic self. Healthy relationships create environments that promote authenticity, acceptance, and encourage personal growth.

Freedom to have a private life: Many people feel entitled to know everything about their partners—all of their thoughts, feelings, and experiences. They believe that a committed relationship gives them license to access their partner's inner life. Some couples manage to balance shared and private domains. Couples need to decide how transparent or private they want to be.

Freedom to have your own friends, adventures, and vacations: Some partners share everything: family, friends, vacations, adventures, etc. They believe that sharing is good and separation is bad. Others feel suffocated by so much sharing, and require more "me" and less "we" time. Couples succeed at every point along the share-all to share-less spectrum.

Freedom to be a multifaceted person: Everyone has many facets to his or her personality. Some facets are active while others remain dormant. Often, some facets contradict one another. A person may be capable of being a sensitive nurturer and a Marine Corps drill sergeant. One partner may refuse to acknowledge or openly disapprove of facets of the other. This can cause the disapproved partner to go underground to feel accepted. Repression causes a person to lose parts of him- herself.

Freedom to change: People change over time. What motivates a twenty-one-year-old probably won't work for a forty-five-year-old. The needs and desires of young couples differ from those in retirement. Ideally, partners encourage and accept change in one another.

Freedom to have your own space: Some couples enjoy sharing the same physical space when they're together. Others like separate offices or bedrooms. The degree of togetherness and separation is negotiable.

Freedom to pursue passions, dreams, and interests: Sometimes a partner has interests his partner does not share. An extreme example of this is a friend of mine who is an avid sailor and takes trips for months at a time. His wife enjoys living alone during these times, and feels that separation reinvigorates their connection. Obviously, few people could accept such an arrangement. Partners can negotiate the amount of "us" time and "me" time they want. The balance depends on what the relationship can tolerate.

Freedom to do what you want, when you want: Does a partner need permission to spend time away? Do partners need to check in? How often? How does having children impact these decisions?

Freedom from your own inner conflict: Almost daily we face conflicts between what we want and what we think we "should" do. Different parts of a person have conflicting motivations. For instance, you might want to take a vacation, but also set aside money for your children's college fund. Perhaps your partner wants to go to the movies. You want to stay home and practice guitar, but you also want to please your partner. What do you decide? We are faced with decisions like this all of the time. When inner conflicts are unexpressed and unresolved, a person may get depressed or suffer from anxiety. When inner conflicts are acknowledged, we can strive for a more harmonious balance.

The clearer we can be about our needs and the nature of our commitment to one another the greater our chances for relationship satisfaction. In the next section we'll discuss the subject of commitment.

What is Commitment?

If you say that you are in a committed relationship, what does that mean? What are you actually committing to? When I ask that question of people who claim to be in committed relationships, they say things like: I'm committed to my partner; I'm committed to loving my partner; We are committed to having a spiritual bond. When I ask for clarification, most people get tongue-tied or mumble words that sound like marriage vows — love, honor, sickness, health.

It's rare for couples to discuss and agree upon shared principles of commitment. Many would be surprised to learn of their partner's definition of commitment. For some, the extent of commitment starts and ends with a promise of monogamy. As long as they aren't having sex with anyone but their partner, they feel they've satisfied their commitment. Never mind that they stonewall their partner, leave their clothes lying around, and show no respect.

People commonly adopt overarching goals and aspirations for themselves in relationships. This is a good start. Here are some commitment gems, culled from forty years of therapy practice, for you to consider:

- ◙ Personal growth of a partner;

- ◙ Remain emotionally engaged with one another;

- ◙ Same level of emotional commitment to the relationship;

- ◙ Health and well-being of your partner;

- ◙ Love, care and support your partner;

- ◙ Work things through and find solutions to problems;

- ◙ Encourage partner to pursue his or her passions;

- ◙ Live by the agreements partners create;

- ◙ Consider partner when making important decisions;

- ◙ Help partner realize dreams.

Defining Commitment

Each couple needs to get serious and define together what they mean by commitment. This process helps you get clear about what you're promising one another. It also brings to the surface your dreams and expectations for the relationship. Abstract principles, like those in the last section, can serve as the umbrella for further specifics. Start by clearly defining what your unique commitment looks like. For each principle, talk about feelings, actions, reactions, expectations, and consequences.

These kinds of talks move you from lofty abstractions and woo-woo vagueness to the real-life stuff where true love lives. The clarity that emerges will reduce the fear and anxiety that is a byproduct of confusion and uncertainty. In turn, your connection will deepen.

Let me illustrate with some examples:

Commitment to love and care for your partner
Specific actions to achieve commitment goal:
Show me that you love me by unexpectedly cooking dinner, send me a sweet tweet, surprise me with small gifts at random times, tell me you love me.

Commitment to the personal growth of your partner
Specific actions to achieve commitment goal:
Talk with me about my dreams and goals. Encourage and support my goals through specific words and actions. Make it easier for me to go to a seminar by taking over my responsibilities while I'm gone. Be willing to sacrifice, if necessary, to help me reach my goals. Cheer me on. I'll do the same for you.

Clarity gets you into the spirit of commitment. By daily small acts of love, you'll demonstrate your commitment and spark and re-spark the passion in your relationship.

The Big Picture: Walking the Tightrope of Freedom and Secure Connection

In my work with couples, freedom often emerges as an area of contention. Couples struggle when one partner's need for a secure connection conflicts with the other partner's desire to feel free. For some, a partner's freedom triggers feelings of insecurity or anxiety.

It's not like the old days, when roles clearly defined the parameters of freedom. In the 21st century, there is no one set of rules. What works for one couple might not work for another. Each couple must negotiate the degree to which they want freedom for themselves and their level of comfort in allowing freedom for their partners.

People naturally desire to be independent and autonomous. We want others to embrace our individuality and uniqueness. We need room to breathe and be ourselves, to think our own thoughts, and feel what we feel without anyone asking us to change or be something we're not. To be your true self in relationship (and to allow your partner to be his or her true self) is one of life's biggest challenges.

But here's the rub: People want freedom, but they also want the security of a committed relationship, like a comfortable pair of slippers you can't wait to put on. We all want love, acceptance, respect, and passion. We want to feel confident that when we wake up in the morning our relationship will be the same as when we went to sleep the night before. We want to feel that our partner's emotional commitment matches our own, and that our connection is solid and predictable.

Over the years, I've been fascinated by the myriad ways couples accommodate their different freedom-security styles. Their arrangements are intricate, and reflect the uniqueness of their individual inner relationship fingerprints (explained in chapter 2) and their relationship. How much freedom do you need in a relationship? How much safety and constancy do you want?

Every couple faces the tension between freedom and the security of commitment. The balance of the two is pivotal to the success of a relationship. A couple reaches equilibrium when both have space enough to feel free yet feel connected enough to feel safe and loved. At this delicate tipping point you are having your cake and eating it too. You luxuriate in the sweet spot.

Julie and Jim have been happily married for ten years. They share office space, friends, and most interests, and rarely spend any time apart. For Chuck, the thought of such togetherness makes him gasp for air. He needs plenty of space to do his own thing, though he adores his wife Lisa. Their time together is limited to dinner on Wednesdays, a date on Saturday night, and a quiet Sunday at home together. In his leisure time, Chuck pursues a life of his own: band practice, playing poker, and golf. An independent guy like Chuck is perfect for Lisa, an ambitious lawyer who works twelve-hour days. She says that men are like pets — you want one around, but not in your face all the time. Lisa loves Chuck's independence and self-sufficiency. She enjoys her own interests, and spends time with her sisters when she's not working.

The arrangements of these two couples work well for them, because their freedom and security needs are compatible. Couples may encounter problems when these needs differ significantly. One partner may feel suffocated while the other grasps for security. Sometimes one partner wants a relationship like Julie and Jim's, and the other partner leans toward a relationship like Chuck and Lisa's. It can be challenging to design a relationship that meets each partner's need for freedom and security.

To better understand the options available to couples in conflict, let's visit the lives of a couple with very different freedom-security styles.

Eva and Jack Struggle to Find the Sweet Spot

Eva, single for the past fifteen years, spent every Friday and Saturday night Salsa dancing. After she started dating Jack, Eva danced less often. As they approached marriage, Jack, eager to please his new wife, decided to take up Salsa. He took the lessons offered before the dance. At these dances everyone circulates, dancing with as many partners as possible. Couples are permitted to dance only the first and last dances together. It was crucial for Jack to learn the steps. After diligent effort and concentration, Jack found he lacked rhythm and grace. He was both out of step and stepping on toes. He struggled for three weeks to emerge from wallflower status, but failed. Jack declared, "That's it—never again!"

Eva faced a dilemma: Leave Jack behind, or give up dancing. At first, she stopped dancing, not wanting to risk Jack's displeasure. After three or four months, Eva was angry and resentful, which intensified as she watched reruns of Jack's favorite action movies or hockey games. Impatient, she made snide remarks. One night she blew up at him: "Next weekend I'm going dancing. It's not my problem that you have two left feet. Being a couch potato is hardly my idea of living."

Feeling demeaned by her words, Jack got furious. Luckily, though, he was more perceptive than his action heroes and did not react. He wanted to clear his own confusion rather than risk compounding the problem. He felt conflicted. He wanted Eva's company, and he wasn't wild about her going dancing alone. He found himself thinking, *What husband "lets" his wife go dancing on Saturday nights without him?*

On the other hand, Jack felt selfish depriving the free-spirited Eva of something she loved. He decided to compromise. He told Eva he'd try to be okay with her dancing a couple of Saturday nights a month, even though a big part of him wanted her home with him. After a few months, Jack learned to handle his discomfort, accept Eva's need for freedom, and let go of his outmoded beliefs about marriage. He organized a group of buddies for solo Saturday sports nights. Eva was grateful for the freedom to pursue her passion without feeling guilty. She admired Jack for working through his conflict. In time Eva and Jack were in the sweet spot—having their cake and eating it too.

Freedom Styles in Relationships

One of the most common maxims about relationships is that opposites attract. In my own experience that is true—sometimes. Like also attracts like. Some people seek a partner who is a mirror image of them. We're all different, and there's no one formula for success.

On the freedom-security continuum, your partner's needs may be similar to or quite different from yours. Let's explore the possible combinations of freedom-security styles and their advantages and disadvantages.

Style 1: Freedom-Freedom Couple

Advantages
Free to live the way they want without pressure;
Each understands the other's need for space;
Share similar desire for spontaneity, stimulation and risk;
Free to be their authentic selves;
Free to pursue their personal dreams;
Free to have their own routines, friends, and other interests.

Disadvantages
Possible loss of connection or intimacy;
Difficulty synchronizing their lives together;
Relationship could lack cohesion.

Style 2: Security-Security Couple

Advantages
Similar needs for constancy and routines;

Neither has desire for high risk or spontaneity;
Emphasis on comfort within relationship;
Good potential for connection and intimacy;
Build dreams together.

Disadvantages
Relationship may feel stale or boring;
Possibility for low passion;
One partner may feel suffocated or stifled.

Style 3: Freedom-Security Couple

Advantages
Partners create a dynamic balance.
Potential to learn from one another;
Partner offers resources to the other to compensate for deficits.

Disadvantages
Differences in approach can be a source of conflict.
Potential for not understanding the other's perspective.

To stay in the sweet spot— maintaining a workable balance of freedom and security— can be elusive. A person's freedom-security style can change over a lifetime. A young person might want more security, and then at a later stage of life want more freedom. For some people, matching their own style with another's might be ideal. Others need the tension of the opposite to keep the juice flowing in the relationship.

Freedom brings with it a kind of insecurity and instability. How much freedom can a relationship tolerate and yet sustain itself? Everyday life tests the boundaries. For instance, is James really comfortable with Kate going out after work for drinks with her boss? Are you comfortable with your partner taking a vacation with friends? Can Jack actually feel good about his Saturday nights alone?

Over the years, I've heard clients complain of stifling relationships. They were bored or felt trapped. When appropriate I recommended, as antidotes for this malady, that they take or give their partners some freedom, be more spontaneous, and live outside their comfort zones. It brings a little edginess, sends a jolt of energy, and reminds the couple that vitality is possible in their relationship — they can have their cake and eat it too.

Chapter 2

Your Inner Relationship Fingerprint

Examine the inside of one of your fingertips. Do you see the intricate pattern of lines? Now imagine each line as a characteristic unique to ...

You
A distinctive constellation of
Needs and wants
Fears, hopes, dread, despair,
Attachment styles,
Delusions, dreams, appetites, thoughts, sensations, sensitivities,
Chemistry, DNA, body type, biorhythms,
Temperament, idiosyncrasies, habits, behaviors,
Strengths, weaknesses, talents, limitations, emotional intelligence,
Chaos, change, intimacy, solitude, emotionality,
Independence, dependence, interdependence,
Masculine, Feminine,
All creating
Your own
Inner Relationship Fingerprint.

You are a unique layering of biology, biography, archetype, culture, and experience. Together these form an intricate system of thoughts, beliefs, habits, feelings, and expectations about relationships. In this book, we call this wondrous pattern your Inner Relationship Fingerprint or "Fingerprint" or "IRF." Like your own fingerprint, your IRF is the only one of its kind. Your inner relationship fingerprint drives your behavior and influences your experience in your relationship. Your IRF is complex, and to a certain extent needs to be deconstructed to be understood. Without some awareness of your IRF, your relationships will be driven by your unconscious. Understanding relationship patterns, problems, and frustrations within the context of your IRF makes change possible and gets you closer to the cake. To better understand this, let's begin by exploring a real-life quandary and see how it happens.

Anna and Greg

Anna and Greg sat silently at opposite ends of the couch. After a few moments I asked, "So, where shall we begin?"

They looked at each other, and then Greg began by matter-of-factly saying, "Anna is cheating on me. She's been having an affair. She hasn't realized that I've known for a while." He then turned to Anna, who was trembling, and continued, "No use denying it. I've followed you for months, and I know firsthand about your rendezvous after work, times at the Blue Hills Motel, and your so-called 'work weekends.' A secret agent you are not."

Anna cried. Then I sensed anger in her words: "Why didn't you say anything? Do you hate me so much you'd embarrass me like this in front of a stranger?"

Greg calmly replied, "To tell you the truth, there never was a right time. I waited and hoped you'd tell me yourself that you planned to leave me for 'Mr. Honda Accord.' Detecting your lies became a little game for me."

"You're such an asshole. I don't know how I've lived with you for so long."

"Hold on—you're the one cheating and destroying our family. And you're calling *me* an asshole?"

Anna's Fingerprint

Anna was the youngest of three children born to first-generation Italian American parents. Her father worked as a landscaper and gardener for wealthy people. Although he put his children through college, he himself never learned to read or write English.

Anna's mother was a homemaker who earned extra money cleaning other peoples' houses part-time. Her parents' relationship was strictly old-world. Her father was in charge. No one would ever dare challenge his authority, though he "ruled" as a benevolent dictator.

Anna watched and learned well the womanly skill of managing husbands. Her mother and her friends believed that all men were buffoons. They manipulated their husbands by regularly stroking their egos, and got nearly everything they wanted.

This strategy worked well for Anna when she was in college and later as a single woman. She never really considered herself manipulative. Her maxim: no harm, no foul.

Books, movies, and TV sitcoms reinforced Anna's beliefs. She loved stories of strong women bending situations to their will, and she especially identified with Scarlet O'Hara, fiction's manipulator extraordinaire.

When, thirteen years ago, Anna married Greg, she assumed that she would train him quickly. And she did. Greg was willing to go along with whatever Anna wanted as long as she behaved as though he was the one calling the shots.

After a decade, Anna felt a gnawing emptiness inside her. Although she appeared to have everything she wanted, including complete control of Greg, she felt despair. Being the puppet master was not all it was cracked up to be. Anna yearned to feel alive again. That was when she began a series of affairs.

Anna recognized at a young age the limitations her family and society placed upon women. Like her mother, Anna tested these family and cultural norms while always staying within their boundaries. When she married Greg, Anna sought to control him; her inner relationship fingerprint was comfortable with this familiar role. Over time, Greg's passivity frustrated Anna, and she grew to disdain his compliance with her demands. Anna faced a conflict between her developing adult self who wanted to be married to her equal and her IRF, which was comfortable with the familiar.

Your IRF as Invisible Writer, Director, and Producer of Your Screenplay

You see in Anna's case how her fingerprint caused her to control her husband and turn him into a passive man for whom she then felt contempt. (Of course, Greg's fingerprint had a role too — he allowed himself to be rendered passive.) It led Anna to seek the excitement she craved by having affairs instead of looking within to see her role in making her relationship less satisfying. No change in her relationship was possible until she gained awareness, knowledge, and mastery over the battle going on inside her. She had not explored her inner relationship fingerprint, so she didn't understand how the influence of her family and culture would affect her behavior and threaten her relationship.

Your IRF influences your relationship experiences in both positive and negative ways. It can limit your capacity to form or sustain satisfying relationships. Since it operates outside your conscious awareness, you, like Anna, might not be sure why you act and react the way you do or why your relationship isn't working. If your life were a screenplay, your IRF would be the invisible writer, director, and producer.

The unconscious power exerted by the inner relationship fingerprint may explain why couples experience feeling suffocated, stifled, trapped, or unloved and unappreciated, without understanding the reason. It may also explain why couples who feel dissatisfied are afraid to admit, even to themselves, that the love they have is nothing like the love they want. It may be why a partner fears that his partner will leave if he stops trying to please her or if he tells her what's really on his mind. Many people feel pressured to change their personality or habits to make their partners happy. Others feel intimidated when their partners change, even for the better. Afraid to risk disconnection, they may distort or lose parts of themselves. These human tendencies make it difficult for a person to be true to himself while also keeping a partner happy.

It's easy to see how couples benefit from awareness of their IRF, and learn of its very personal and powerful impact. Let's face it: love is a messy game with no guarantees, yet love is also the most profound and satisfying experience in a lifetime. By becoming aware of your IRF, real and lasting change becomes possible, and with the ability to change, you increase your chances of relationship success.

Is your curiosity piqued? If your answer is yes, it's the right time for you to explore your inner relationship fingerprint. As a first step, visit www.freeandconnected.com/fingerprint where you will find an eighty-question assessment to take. You will discover which of four distinct types best describes you, and get a general idea — the broad brushstrokes — of your fingerprint. As you progress through part 1 of this book, you will learn about the fine detail and intricacies of your particular fingerprint and understand how it has shaped your relationships so far. After you've completed the assessment, return to this page and reread the descriptions of the four fingerprint types.

Use the following prompts to consider and record your thoughts and feelings about the results.

Your Inner Relationship Fingerprint Type

Your Inner Relationship Fingerprint is unique to you — no one else has an exact replica. By taking the 80-question assessment, you discovered which of the four distinct types best describes you and got a general idea of your fingerprint. As you progress through part 1 of our book, you will deepen your understanding of the impact of your fingerprint on your close relationships.

The following is a description of the four fingerprint types: Red, Yellow, Blue, and Green. Awareness of your type will give you new perspective about your relationship style. Familiarity with the four types will help you to identify the fingerprint type of those closest to you.

Red

Red screams dominance in your close relationships. Red feels self-confident and uncompromising (except in business). Red can be calculating, tactless, and intimidating. Everyone, especially your partner, takes notice when Red's muscles get flexed. On the other hand, Red is fun-loving and spontaneous.

Red loves freedom and adventure, and feels compelled to take risks. In relationships, Red wants new challenges to satisfy, mountains to climb. Red energy can make monogamy and fidelity difficult, particularly in a lackluster, routine relationship where Red feels stuck.

In crisis, Red courageously protects and defends loved ones.

Red is tenacious and confident that he or she can slay whatever problems life presents.

Never a person who likes to be told what to do, Red resists authority or supervision from anyone, including, and sometimes especially, his or her partner. Red is competent: a can-do person who knows how to do things or will figure it out on his or her own. Red personifies the qualities of determination, harnessed energy, and resourcefulness.

But remember: Red must guard against potential rigidity and closing off from what others have to offer. Red does not hold the patent on good ideas and creativity.

Red alternates between exuberant social butterfly and cave-dwelling introvert. These extremes can cause moodiness and confuse those around Red. Also, Red prefers a direct communication style, which at times can be harsh, hurtful, and/or insensitive. Red gets surprised when someone mistakes Red's abundant self-confidence for arrogance—a blind spot that can interfere with Red's relationships.

Red is quick-witted. Red dominates decision making in relationships, which often results in an imbalance of power. Red needs to curb self-righteousness and/or unbending behavior with partners. Partners need to feel that Red listens to and considers their ideas.

Red's energy is dynamic and positive in relationships. Use caution that you don't sabotage your relationships by your need for control.

Yellow

Yellow is security minded, seeking comfort and constancy in relationships. Yellow likes to believe that things will be the same tomorrow as they are today. Yellow prefers order, set routines, and a structured life. Risk, adventure, and experimentation do not interest Yellow.

Yellow is a team player, willing to sublimate personal needs and wants for the betterment of relationships. Yellow can be a rock of support. Yellow rejoices when a partner succeeds, and fully shares in the accomplishment. Yellows can become so entwined with their partners that they risk losing themselves.

Yellow can be indecisive. Even when Yellows know what they want, they try to calculate a positive outcome for everyone involved in a situation. This sort of complex analysis can be overwhelming and make decision making thorny and slow.

Yellow is a social creature, yet also shy by nature. Yellow can also be introverted. The idea of closing out the world and curling up with a book appeals to Yellow too.

Yellow often seeks a mentor or a teacher. Sometimes a partner may fill that role. Yellows tend to choose a partner whose strengths and abilities complement their own. Yellow finds comfort in the knowledge that a partner is reliable and will stand up for him or her when necessary.

Blue

Above all, Blue wants a soul mate—a partner who loves, understands, and accepts the authentic Blue. Blue wants to be completely open with a mate. Blue imagines a relationship to be like riding a bicycle built for two, the partners pedal through life in tandem.

Blue exerts great effort to maintain a dynamic sense of balance in relationships. With all the pressures and turmoil of modern life, this is no easy feat. Egalitarian relationships are challenging. Sometimes Blue may seek the comfort of a dominant or submissive role, but like an invisible scale, Blue pushes toward the center, back to love and authenticity.

A relationship between Blues is characterized by fluidity. Success requires frequent and good communication to maintain symmetry. Each move (or change) by one requires a coordinated move (or change) by the other. Roles and responsibilities, i.e., parenting, housework, wage earning, are less fixed and more changeable.

Blue's high expectations make Blue quite demanding. Any imbalance in relationship causes Blue to sound an alarm and feel dissatisfied. Blue is big on process. As a result, Blue requires continual dialogue, negotiation, and compromise in relationship—a process that may be tiring for other types.

Green

Green focuses on survival. Green's ability to adapt is phenomenal, and is an asset in relationships. Green is an expert at analyzing and interpreting the expectations of others. Without losing a beat, Green can instantly make internal adjustments and satisfy another's expectations.

Green embodies versatility and flexibility, making it easy to connect with different kinds of people. Greens quickly evaluate interpersonal situations, and call upon the resonant part of themselves. Green has the ability to make nuanced changes as circumstances require. Green's adaptability remains a strength as long as Green remembers to hang onto his or her real self. Green must be careful not to lose track of who he or she really is.

Green is highly imaginative and enjoys fantasy. When a relationship struggles, Green visualizes how it can be improved. Green can be a restless soul. Dissatisfaction with partners is common. Green has bouts of envy about other couple's relationships. Green can be a discontent and struggle with acceptance of self and others, which can make for a tumultuous relationship and life.

Green can be a dreamer or a visionary in relationships (as well as a flirt). Green must be intentional and use this transformational energy constructively.

Now that you have discovered your fingerprint type and

read the descriptions, use the following prompts to consider and record your thoughts and feelings about the results.

Review and Reflection:
Interpreting Your Fingerprint

1. In what ways do you think your fingerprint type captures your relationship style?

_____

_____

_____

2. Were there any aspects of your fingerprint type that did not resonate for you?

_____

_____

_____

3. How do you feel about your dominant aspect (i.e., I am glad to be Red. I am a kick-ass guy)?

_____

_____

_____

4. Which aspects of your fingerprint type would you like to adjust? Why?

_____

_____

_____

5. Did anything about your fingerprint type surprise you? Why or why not?

_____

_____

_____

In what ways does your fingerprint type positively affect your relationship?

_____

_____

_____

In what ways does your fingerprint type limit your relationship?

_____

_____

_____

Chapter 3

Time to Shift the Focus to YOU

If, like most people, what you really want to do is fix your relationship right now, why are you asked to focus on yourself? You know what the problems are, and if your partner would change, so would your relationship. You're probably thinking: *Why start from square one? Let's get to the meat of the matter.* Don't worry, you will, but not quite yet. If you keep an open mind, take a small leap of faith, and read on, we will take you on a journey that promises to give you clarity and reinvigorate your relationship.

I know it might seem counterintuitive to restrict the focus to yourself, but I assure you that this method really works. Here's why: Your chances for a stronger and more vibrant relationship improve greatly when you know yourself from the inside out. This is true because the better you know yourself the healthier and more whole you become. And the healthier and more whole you are the healthier your relationship will be. Healthy relationships are built by self-aware, intentional individuals who understand who they are, what they want, and what holds them back from getting it.

Tune in to WYOU: Your Inner Radio Broadcast

Take your time with the next exercise and with all of the exercises in this book. You are gathering vital information about your unique self. Go at your own pace, pause along the way, and revisit any bumps you encounter along the road. You might decide to go only part of the way. Remember: You are in the driver's seat. Relax. It's all about you, after all!

Everyone has a personal radio station playing in his or her head. WYOU broadcasts messages exclusively to you twenty-four hours a day, seven days a week. Did you know that the average person thinks approximately 50,000 thoughts per day? The lion's share of these relates to your own value, potential, performance, and ability. And guess what? In case WYOU isn't oppressive enough already, most of these messages are negative and they replay over and over until you believe them as truth.

Here's an example of how this works. I was extremely hyperactive as a child. Never able to keep still, I was the sort of impulsive, inattentive, fidgety child who drives adults crazy. Sitting at a desk in school for six hours a day was torture.

These were the unenlightened days before psychologists and educators knew about ADHD (attention deficit hyperactivity disorder). Needless to say, I was in constant trouble both at home and in school. I wasn't bad, just annoying, always moving, tapping my fingers, and talking a blue streak. No one understood that I couldn't control these behaviors. In my perpetual overdrive my motor kept running after I was told to shut it off and had tried to.

You can imagine the steady torrent of negative messages fired at me by parents, teachers, and other adults. I soon accepted that I was irresponsible, thoughtless, and pretty much good for nothing. I believed the things people told me about myself. These negative messages played on my inner radio broadcast all the time.

It wasn't until college and after I'd matured that I developed strategies to harness my excess energy. Then, with increased exposure and experience to an ever-widening world—college, then jobs, then graduate school—I discovered that these negative messages about me actually weren't true. Gradually, the old negative labels got replaced with a more realistic picture. With effort and a little help from others, I shed most of the negative messages. I felt lighter and happier.

Everyone can benefit from facing down his or her negative radio broadcast. In the next section, you'll explore the ways the broadcast impacts our thoughts, feelings, and behaviors in relationships.

Core Beliefs — The Dialogue between Your Conscious Mind and Your Deepest Self

These messages, which psychologists call core beliefs, are a dialogue between your conscious mind and your deepest self. Formed in childhood, these core beliefs shape your perceptions of yourself and your place in the world. You have core beliefs about your self-worth, lovability, attractiveness, character, and potential.

Your core beliefs form your self-image and worldview. Everything that you experience gets filtered to fit what you already believe. This can create a huge obstacle to expanding your self-perception through new experiences. Often your beliefs need to change to let new experiences slip in through the cracks.

If, for example, January believes she's plain and unappealing to men, then when Ben flirts with her she probably won't interpret his actions as flirting; rather, she believes that Ben feels sorry for her. Ava, on the other hand, knows she is intelligent. When her boss presents a challenging assignment, Ava will be confident of her inevitable success.

Your inner radio broadcasts your core beliefs on your dedicated channel WYOU. For the most part you screen it out. Otherwise, you couldn't function in the world. But notice what happens on a bad day: Negative thoughts flood your mind when things aren't going well, like when your boss criticizes you in front of all your coworkers. Do you latch onto the most negative thought and let it take you for a ride down a wormhole? On these days when you feel vulnerable, hurt, depressed, or lonely, it gets more difficult to tune out negative messages. They seem to circle your head like vultures.

Even when the volume is down, a steady hum reaches you. The broadcast sends a stream of messages from your deepest self. This constant barrage influences your mood, thoughts, and behavior, mostly outside your awareness. These unconscious messages cause people to do and say perplexing things that they sometimes later regret. By tuning in to your inner radio and learning the program lineup, you can gradually liberate yourself from this kind of unaware behavior. The more you listen, the more discerning you'll become about the accuracy and inaccuracy of the messages. To help with this process, I teach my clients a simple practice. As a negative message arises they can test its truth by asking themselves: *What is the evidence to support this message?* It can be amazing how quickly negative messages disappear.

Exercise 2: Tune In

For one week tune into WYOU and monitor the messages you hear. Complete the chart below, and then label each message as positive or negative. I guarantee that with this kind of hyper-focus you will eradicate many of those unconscious pests.

WYOU Message Log

Message	Positive	Negative	Evidence
I am irresponsible.		✕	*I forgot to pay my electric bill. BUT … I work every day, and I usually pay my bills on time. Conclusion: I am actually a responsible person.*

Review and Reflection — WYOU

What kinds of things do you say to yourself? Do you call yourself names like idiot, slob, lazybones, or loser? Or do you say things like I'm hot, a great dresser, clever, and so hilarious? Begin to notice patterns of message activity throughout your day. As you do, you can use these questions to help you to focus on the messages:

Is the flow of your messages positive or negative?

_____

_____

Does it depend on the particular day or your activity?

_____

_____

Do the messages change with the company you keep?

_____

_____

Are you harsh with yourself?

_____

_____

Do you tend to be critical of others?

_____

_____

Do particular people, places or things trigger certain messages?

_____

_____

How do you react to the triggered messages?

_____

_____

_____

_____

What feelings do they evoke?

_____

_____

_____

Do you believe that the messages are true?

_____

_____

_____

Still-Point Meditation

Let's start learning about your *still point,* the quiet place inside you where you are free of turmoil, self-judgment, and real-life pressures. Your still point is the home of your deepest self, a place of perfect tranquility.

In the still point you let go of thinking and create spaciousness in your mind. As thoughts intrude, you gently label them "thoughts" and watch them drift away. You move to a calmer, more neutral place. You dwell in inner peace without conflict. In the still point, your anxiety and fear lift.

Moving to the still point helps you unlock your unconscious and access an expanded awareness of yourself. Your unconscious holds untold treasures that reveal themselves when you are ready. Your unconscious communicates with you nightly when you dream. Through dreams you integrate unconscious material with your conscious mind.

So, are you ready to go to this comforting, gentle space? Before you actually start, read the instructions below.

Going to Your Still Point

Sit in a comfortable chair, or if you prefer, lie down (if you can stay awake). Choose a quiet place where you won't be disturbed. Arrange your body in a relaxed position. You'll be sitting or reclining for ten to fifteen minutes.

Take some slow, deep breaths, as many as you need. Let the breath fill every part of your body as you inhale, and feel a sense of tranquility. As you exhale, let go of all stress, tension, and pressure. Feel it leaving your body. Blow it all out. Keep breathing this way until you are completely relaxed. There is nowhere to go and nothing to do. The only thing that matters is this moment, right now. Give yourself this time to simply be—just you, and no one else. Feel how good it is to let go, even for just a few moments. If you feel tension in any areas of your body, ask them to let go and relax. Relax your hands, arms, shoulders, neck, jaw, lips, and the space between your eyebrows. Try to resist any distraction; when thoughts enter in your mind (and they will), return to your breathing, inhale relaxation and peace, and exhale away all tension. Let the thoughts drift away like autumn leaves floating lightly on a stream. Feel your heartbeat and your blood circulate, nourishing the cells in your body. Connect with your deepest self—you are in the still point. Keep breathing. Stay there as long as you feel comfortable.

Benefits of Still-Point Practice

Commit to do this practice a couple of times a day, ideally for fifteen minutes. If you're short on time, five minutes will do. Daily practice will provide many benefits: You'll be more relaxed. You'll notice your thoughts and sensations and the pushes and pulls you feel in your daily interactions. Your powers of observation will get keener. You'll become more self-confident, more connected with yourself, and experience less anxiety and fear. With continued practice, creative ideas start to percolate, and joy surfaces from your deepest parts. Hallelujah!

To start, simply notice what comes up for you. Use your breath to turn down the volume of your inner radio broadcast. Your thoughts drift away like puffy white clouds sweeping across the sky.

As you practice shifting the focus to *you,* and spend longer periods of time in your still point, your deeper feelings and beliefs begin to emerge. You develop a more intimate connection with your inner landscape. Through this process you'll become better acquainted with your inner relationship fingerprint and discover how it shaped you. As you move through the exercises, you'll work with strong emotions, some of which are corrosive to relationships. You'll begin to let go of anger, disappointment, and guilt. You'll dissolve distorted thinking, puncture myths, and reframe expectations to better fit the person you are today.

As already stated, but well worth repeating, the irony is that when you shift the focus to yourself, your ultimate reward is a deeper, more robust, and lasting connection with your partner. You'll get the kind of relief that feels like taking off very tight shoes after a five-mile walk.

A word for singles: Don't worry if you don't have a partner today. Synchronistically, people attract partners after gaining greater clarity about who they are and what they want. It opens a space for new love.

Master of Your Domain

Simply by living on this blue planet, you get to know yourself by trial and error. People make mistakes, stumble and pick themselves up, fall in and out of love, break hearts and get their hearts broken. You know more about yourself than anyone else does. But having said that, everyone has blind spots. This comes from living in your own skin. All the messages you receive in your early years are grooved into your neural pathways. Subsequent messages deepen the groove. We know that many of the messages are not accurate. Often, your perception about yourself is distorted and lacks objectivity.

Through the strategies in this book, your clarity about yourself will grow sharper than a high-definition image, lighting the path for a more satisfying relationship. Why wait for relationship happiness when you can jump-start the process?

In the exercises up to this point, you tuned into the deepest parts of yourself. Perhaps you discovered new aspects of your personality and behavior. Maybe you met head-on certain traits you've spent a lifetime trying to ignore. For example, at times you've been cruel to someone, unfeeling, or unforgiving.

As you notice your own thoughts, emotions, and behavior, you'll get to know yourself in a deeper way. You'll access the full spectrum of your emotions — your joy and sadness, anger and fear, love and hate. You'll notice your conflicted impulses to be generous/petty, kind/cruel, loving/angry, and peaceful/anxious. You'll learn firsthand how these contradictory forces cause inner tension, which drains your energy and lead to anxiety or depression.

Self-knowledge is power. By getting a better grasp of your inner landscape, you'll get to know your "hot buttons." Instead of acting on impulse, you can slow down the action and exert control. You can reflect on a thought or feeling, and, before you react, ask yourself: *What is going on here?* You might decide not to react to a given situation. With practice, the skills of self-focus and reflection will be woven into your everyday experience. Then, you will truly be the master of your domain.

Bella and Ed

Let's drop in on Bella and Ed. You'll see how Bella's new self-awareness sparks change in their relationship. Bella cried during our first session as she told me about her marriage. She described the relationship as a mixture of sadness, frustration, and regret. She told me that Ed was demanding and emotionally needy. He had just ended a painful relationship when they met.

After six years, Bella grew tired of taking care of Ed. His victimhood repulsed her. She felt she couldn't turn to him for comfort when she needed it. When she did try, he would divert the conversation back to himself. Bella spent our session railing about her husband's words, actions, and accusations. Toward the end, I asked her about her role in Ed's problems. She stared at me blankly. It was apparent that she was far more aware of Ed's needs and wants than her own.

Initially, I encouraged Bella to shift her focus away from her husband and to herself—no easy task. We spent several sessions identifying what she wanted and needed for herself. In the process, Bella realized that she no longer wanted to play the role of Ed's mother. She recognized her need for an adult relationship with more mutuality. Bella understood that her need to rescue Ed was a compensation for her fear that she was not a nurturing person. As a child her mother had told her repeatedly that she cared only about herself and that she was selfish.

In our sessions, we talked about how long-term relationships go through different stages, and how a person's needs and wants change over time. Bella recognized that at this point in her life she occasionally wanted someone to take care of her. She wanted the security of knowing that she could rely on Ed to take charge sometimes. Bella was relieved when she realized that she was no longer compelled to prove she was generous and caring.

Bella and I decided that it would be helpful to include Ed for a few sessions, so that the three of us would have an opportunity to integrate Bella's realizations into their relationship. Ed, who was tall and had red hair and a freckled complexion, was shy and soft-spoken. When Ed, born in Ukraine, was five years old, an American family adopted him from an orphanage. Although the family had been very kind, Ed no longer maintained consistent contact with them. Bella was his only real family and the only person in the world he really cared about. He agreed that their relationship was not going well, and he felt motivated to save it.

Wishy-washy, Mixed Messages Dilute the Power of You

We all send mixed messages from time to time. We say one thing and mean another. Our facial expressions contradict our words. Our body language speaks volumes, embellishing a simple statement.

Linguists agree that words account for only a tiny percentage of communication. Messages are also communicated by body language, facial expression, vocal tone, and other qualities of voice. Mixed messages pose a problem for the receiver, who gets confused and sometimes feels the need to ask for clarification.

What makes people send mixed messages? Mixed messages reflect internal conflict in the speaker. For instance, Janet's husband informed her that he had reserved Sunday mornings to play golf with his buddies. The words stung, and Janet wasn't sure why. A part of her wanted to be a good sport and support her mate's interest. Another part of Janet felt hurt, taken for granted, and abandoned. She questioned whether she had the right to restrict her husband's freedom. To avoid a knockdown-dragout argument, she opted to encourage his choice.

But Janet's inner struggle continued. It left her in turmoil each Sunday as she kissed her husband goodbye with the sadness of a five-year-old girl on her face. After a couple of weeks, Janet's husband picked up on the mixed nature of the message. He asked Janet if she *really* felt okay about his golf. He told her how sad she looked when she said goodbye, leading him to feel it wasn't all right. Janet admitted to her feelings of hurt and abandonment. She asked her husband to consider changing his golf dates to every other Sunday and to plan a couple of weekends at the seashore together. He agreed. Later in the summer, when Janet realized her mate was missing his favorite tournament, she urged him to play even though it was an off weekend.

A 5-Step Strategy —
Saying What You Mean with Clarity

Step 1: Before uttering a mixed message or shaky communication, take a few moments. You can always count to ten or take several breaths before speaking. Search inside yourself for areas of rebellion, rumbling, or contradiction. Explore how an inner conflict might feel in your body. For instance, your throat might feel dry, your chest tight, or your palms sweaty. If you feel conflicted, you might need more time before you speak. Let me give you a trick that therapists use to buy time when unsure how to respond. They ask the client, "Can you say more about that?" Try it. (In Janet's case, she could've stalled for time by asking what the golf dates meant to her husband.)

Step 2: Decide whether you're clear about what you are communicating. If you're still uneasy, try to identify the source. You mighty still feel uncertain or confused and not ready for the solution (Janet had the option to postpone her response to her husband until she was ready.)

Step 3: The decision about whether to share your inner conflict is always yours. Carefully consider the time, place and likely reaction of the receiver of your communication. (Janet could decide to share her inner conflict to help her husband understand her mixed messages.)

Step 4: Explore your anxiety at sharing your inner conflict. Is it based on a fear of rejection, ridicule, or abandonment? (Janet had the option of searching her past for similar experiences to help her understand her strong reaction.)

Step 5: If you decide to share your inner conflict, you could open with something like "I find that I'm having some mixed feelings about what you're saying. I wonder if we can talk about this some more." (Janet and her husband have the option to discuss Janet's conflict if she feels intimate enough with him.)

Bella and Ed (continued)

Several months later, Bella and Ed reconvened in my office. Bella tearfully admitted that she had been giving Ed mixed messages for some time. While she often told him that she loved him, she also avoided his company whenever possible. The contradiction between Bella's words and actions confused Ed and made him more needy and demanding.

Bella worked on clearly and honestly articulating what she wanted for herself—an adult relationship with a man who would take care of her sometimes. Ed began to grasp that some of his behaviors were driving Bella away. He admitted that he too had been sending mixed messages about his role as victim. He wasn't as needy as he portrayed, but expressed his fear of losing her. As a victim he felt secure she'd stay with him. It turned out that each of them was carrying on with the roles that first attracted them to one another. They fell into a rescuer-victim pattern that took hard work to break, and, as a result of their newfound clarity, they changed in ways that leveled the playing field and drastically improved their relationship.

Chapter 4

Family—Your First Imprint

Nancy

In this chapter you'll read a case study that's more comprehensive and detailed than the previous ones. Nancy's story illustrates the power a woman's inner relationship fingerprint exerts on her personality, relationships, and life.

Nancy walked into her first session with a look of terror on her face. She was forty years old, impeccably dressed, and well groomed, with not a hair out of place. She told me she had been depressed for as long as she could remember.

In a trembling voice Nancy said, "I've always been able to separate the areas of my life into compartments. I don't let my problems interfere with work, but lately it's been tougher." Nancy worked as the chief financial officer of a startup technology company. She told me that she had always felt comfortable with the predictability of numbers. "The job is very demanding, long hours, work on weekends. I'm not complaining, but it does take most of my energy."

"So what isn't working?"

"I am a complete disappointment to my family. I feel guilty all the time. My husband, Alan, got laid off a couple of years ago. Now that he's home, he's become the primary parent of our teenage daughter. When I leave for work, I feel like I'm abandoning them."

"So, you're the family breadwinner?"

"Well, yeah, I've supported us for a while. Actually, my husband hasn't had much luck with jobs. He keeps getting let go. I guess he isn't what you might call career oriented."

"Do you resent being the breadwinner?"

"No, but I wish they didn't make me feel so guilty. They used to ask me why I had to work so much, as if they wanted me around. Now they don't even bother. They just look at me like I'm a stranger."

Without any apparent resentment, Nancy told me she also did all the cooking, cleaning, and laundry for the family. She looked up at me and said, "It's busy, but I manage."

Nancy was the eldest of five children. Her alcoholic father had been physically abusive at times. Periodically, her mother would throw him out. Then he'd get sober and send the family priest to beg her mother's forgiveness for him. He'd stay sober for a few months, and then go on another bender, repeating his cycle. When Nancy was in college, her father died in a car accident. His blood alcohol at the time was .27.

Nancy's mother, who taught second grade, provided the emotional and financial stability in the family. She tried to create a consistent and nurturing home environment. A stoic woman, she never spoke ill of her husband. Nancy didn't remember having any real relationship with her father. She started caring for her siblings when she was six. She was mother's little helper, and seemingly had somehow been born competent.

As a teenager she vowed to become an entirely self-sufficient adult. She swore never to find herself in her mother's position, dependent on a man.

"In my twenties I dated a number of men and had sex with a few of them. It's weird. Most of them were like me, bright, ambitious, and career-oriented. Somehow I just couldn't get comfortable. It's as if their confidence and self-assurance intimidated me. I didn't know who or how to be. I felt unprepared, totally clueless. Then I met Peter."

"Peter?"

"Peter was my first real boyfriend. I was twenty-three. We lived together for about six months. I should say I supported him for six months. I worked; he played video games and drank beer with his friends. It was too much like my parents' home. It freaked me out, so I ended the relationship.

"Next there was Simon, a nice-enough guy who even had a job as a cartographer. But a real head case, very neurotic. Every night he whined about the daily indignities he endured. He made Woody Allen seem like the Dalai Lama."

In our work together, Nancy recognized how her parents had unwittingly trained her to be a caretaker and the role became a dominant element in her inner relationship fingerprint. Both Nancy and her mother took care of others while disregarding their own needs.

"I thought Alan, my husband, was different. He had a good sense of humor, didn't seem self-centered or needy, and rarely drank. He seemed like a *mensch*. After our daughter was born, Alan became needier and less able to manage on his own." Nancy shook her head in self-disgust. "I don't know how I could have let this happen. I promised myself I would never be like my mother. I am so angry with myself."

Nancy had been turning a lifetime of unexpressed rage inward. Her rage was then converted into depression. Unconsciously, she was angry with her parents for having made her a "parentified" child and robbed her of a childhood. She was angry with her father for being an absent, alcoholic parent. She was angry at her mother for having five children and staying with a man like her father. She felt angry with the men who wanted her to take care of them but gave her nothing in return. She was angry with her husband and daughter for having to be their caretaker. Through a torrent of tears, Nancy said, "I don't want to become an angry woman."

I suggested that she invite Alan for a few sessions. I was surprised that Alan, who was tall, and had white hair and a healthy, ruddy complexion, appeared to be a decade older than Nancy. He told me that over the last eight years he and Nancy had become increasingly distant.

"She is married to her career and has withdrawn from us. Many nights when she gets home she goes straight to her bedroom. I've only stayed for our daughter. Nancy and I have no life together. I'm sure she told you how she does all the housework. I want you to know that she does, but she insists on it. If I do anything, she gets really angry and critical. It makes her feel better to take care of everything. I suppose it alleviates her guilt, so I let her."

I sensed that, despite the years of anger and distance, Nancy and Alan remained connected to one another. It turned out that they were both invested enough in their marriage to make them willing to work things out.

We began to identify what each of them needed and wanted. Alan wanted to contribute to the family. Ironically, he wanted to take charge of the house, to shop, cook, and clean. Predictably, Nancy did not easily relinquish her domestic chores. She had internalized her mother's caretaker role, but ultimately, having been released from that role, Nancy no longer felt taken advantage of by her family.

In the months that followed, Nancy reported less depression. She and Alan experienced a renewed vitality in their relationship. Nancy even let him take care of her. It was the first time she had had that experience. The couple was on the road to a more satisfying relationship, free of anger, guilt, and old emotional baggage.

People commonly fall into patterns like Nancy did. For instance, women with alcoholic fathers, despite their best intentions, tend to gravitate towards alcoholic partners. Men partnered with highly critical women are likely to repeat the pattern in their next relationship. Women with a history of abuse tend to pair up again with an abusive partner. In a strange way, people get attracted to inappropriate partners for the comfort they find in the familiar, even if it's painful. These patterns get embedded in, and form the intricate design unique to, a person's inner relationship fingerprint.

You might wonder whether it's possible to break out of repetitive patterns. With self-focus and intentionality, you absolutely can! To break a destructive pattern, you need to identify the bad seed at its root. Your parents taught you the basics of self-care and survival, shaped your early socialization, and controlled the arena in which you developed. Your family, good or bad, right or wrong, left a deep imprint on you, which formed your inner relationship fingerprint.

If you grew up in a kind and loving family, your IRF likely integrated those dynamics. If, on the other hand, you grew up in a chaotic environment filled with conflict and turmoil, you probably internalized those characteristics. Of course there are many exceptions. And the good news is that you can get beyond the negative imprints. The exercises in part 1 will deepen your understanding and give you courage to break through patterns.

Your Family — Your History

Here's a chance to visit your childhood, with an eye toward better understanding the underpinnings of your inner relationship fingerprint.

Before you respond to the questions below, spend some time immersing yourself in your childhood. Visualize the house where you grew up. To spark memories, picture yourself in your mind as a child at age five, ten, or fifteen. Take out the family photographs, and really look into your own eyes and those of your family members. When you feel fully steeped in your childhood and family life, your mental state is prepared for the next exercise. Feel free to check more than one response to any question.

I grew up with these people (add each one's name):

❑ Mother _____

❑ Father _____

❑ Step-parent(s) _____

❑ Aunts and Uncles _____

❑ Grandparents _____

❑ Sisters _____

❑ Brothers _____

❑ Others _____
_____

My most vivid memories of my childhood are:

❑ Happy and carefree

❑ Warm memories with my family

❑ Scary and unsafe

❑ Feeling uncertain or confused

❑ Being yelled at or scolded

❑ Devil's food cakes

As a child, my parents/caregivers treated me in a way that was:

❏ Kind and loving

❏ Strict disciplinarians

❏ Able to set clear limits and responsibilities

❏ Easily angered and explosive

❏ Unpredictable

The adult relationship I observed as a child in our home is best characterized as:

❏ Harmonious

❏ Tumultuous with frequent conflict

❏ Unpredictable, with episodes of domestic abuse

❏ Cold and unloving

❏ Cohesive

❏ Other

When I got into trouble as a child, my parent(s) would generally:

❏ Lecture me

❏ Spank me

❏ Humiliate me in front of others

❏ Punish me

❏ Ground me

❏ Do nothing or ignore it

My parent(s) treated my siblings and me:

❑ Equally and fairly

❑ Unequally—I was not the favorite

❑ Unequally—I was the favorite and got all of the cake

❑ Equally and horribly

❑ I'm not sure

Vacations were events that my family:

❑ Dreaded

❑ Enjoyed being together

❑ Never went on together

❑ Were unpredictable

❑ Looked forward to

❑ Turned into nightmares

One or both of my parents used alcohol and drugs:

❑ Excessively

❑ Socially

❑ Rarely

❑ Problematically

❑ Never

From my childhood perspective, it seemed to me that my parents/caregivers:

❑ Loved each other

❏ Had once loved each other

❏ Did not like or respect each other

❏ Lived as separately as possible

❏ Probably never loved each other

If there was one thing that would make my parent(s)
angry it was

_____

_____

Growing up, I felt closest to my:

❏ Mother

❏ Father

❏ Sibling

❏ Other

❏ No one

In my family, the most important thing was:

_____

_____

If there was one lesson I learned from my family it was:

_____

_____

In retrospect, I would describe the way my parent(s)
prepared me for adulthood as:

❏ Helpful

❏ Confusing

❑ A hindrance

❑ Mixed

❑ I'm not sure

My current relationship with my family is:

❑ Nonexistent

❑ Warm and loving

❑ Friendly but distant

❑ Cyclical, with good and bad periods

❑ Very close

❑ I'm not sure

Review and Reflection:
Your Experience of Family

In therapy people often start to remember things they had for-gotten. One memory triggers another and so on. Our memories of events are selective. Memories of traumatic events are often repressed. The family history exercise took you back and helped you to recall the nature and qualities of your childhood family. Being present to these memories will deepen your understand-ing of your inner relationship fingerprint.

In reviewing your responses, you'll begin to connect the dots. You might notice some long-running themes, or changes resulting from major events—the birth of a sibling, relocation, or divorce. The impact of parents on each person varies, even for children in the same family. If you have siblings, you've undoubtedly noticed that their experience and memories of your family are different from your own. Sometimes it's hard to believe that two people grew up in the same family.

When you gain awareness of the impact of your family history, you grow more intimate with yourself. You gain perspective about your struggle with and capacity for romantic relationships. Over time, you make peace with your early history. Only then can your inner relationship fingerprint be transformed.

Chapter 5

Attachment Styles and Your Inner Relationship Fingerprint

In this chapter, you will discover and explore your attachment style, which is a fundamental aspect of your inner relationship fingerprint. An attachment style is a way of behaving in relationships that's made up of three factors: genetic predisposition (your DNA), early experience with parents, and romantic relationships. Your attachment style becomes your mode of relating with your partner and the other significant people in your life.

Researchers in this field have identified three distinct types of attachment styles: Secure, Avoidant, and Anxious/Ambivalent. These three styles will be described shortly, but first there's a quiz for you to take. Are you ready to discover your attachment style?

Which is Your Attachment Style?

This thirty-question quiz is based on several different assessment instruments used by researchers. Identifying and learning about your attachment style will help you understand its effect on your choice of partner, your behavior, and the prevailing dynamic in your relationship. The scoring for this exercise is in the appendix to this book. You can take the assessment online at www.freeandconnected.com, which we recommend for the ease of automatic scoring. Hand scoring for this exercise can be tedious.

1. It's easy for me to be affectionate with my partner (check the appropriate space).
   ○ Agree ○ Disagree ○ Neutral/Mixed

2. I feel that my partner truly understands me.
   ○ Agree ○ Disagree ○ Neutral/Mixed

3. I don't worry about my partner abandoning me.
   ○ Agree ○ Disagree ○ Neutral/Mixed

4. I feel uncomfortable when my partner is vulnerable and reveals emotions.
   ○ Agree ○ Disagree ○ Neutral/Mixed

5. I find it is easy to get close to partners.
   ○ Agree ○ Disagree ○ Neutral/Mixed

6. I can talk to my partner about my problems and concerns.
   ○ Agree ○ Disagree ○ Neutral/Mixed

7. My love relationships are often shallow and lacking intimacy.
   ○ Agree ○ Disagree ○ Neutral/Mixed

8. I am often comfortable relying on my partner.
   ○ Agree ○ Disagree ○ Neutral/Mixed

9. I am confident my partner cares for me.
   ○ Agree ○ Disagree ○ Neutral/Mixed

10. I am uncomfortable getting too close to my partner.
    ○ Agree ○ Disagree ○ Neutral/Mixed

11. I get nervous when my partner gets too close.
○ Agree ○ Disagree ○ Neutral/Mixed

12. I worry my partner does not love me as much as I love him/her.
○ Agree ○ Disagree ○ Neutral/Mixed

13. I find it difficult to depend on my partner.
○ Agree ○ Disagree ○ Neutral/Mixed

14. I pull away when my partner tries to get too close.
○ Agree ○ Disagree ○ Neutral/Mixed

15. I feel uncomfortable sharing my thoughts and feelings with my partner.

○ Agree ○ Disagree ○ Neutral/Mixed

16. I find it difficult to trust romantic partners.
○ Agree ○ Disagree ○ Neutral/Mixed

17. I can go to my partner in times of stress.
○ Agree ○ Disagree ○ Neutral/Mixed

18. I often make excuses to avoid spending time with my partner.
○ Agree ○ Disagree ○ Neutral/Mixed

19. I need my partner to constantly show that he/she really loves me.
○ Agree ○ Disagree ○ Neutral/Mixed

20. I can share my feelings and thoughts with my partner.
○ Agree ○ Disagree ○ Neutral/Mixed

21. I prefer to be in a relationship than not in one.
○ Agree ○ Disagree ○ Neutral/Mixed

22. I want to be very close to my partner – this desire scares me.
○Agree ○Disagree ○Neutral/Mixed

23. My partner understands my emotional needs.
○Agree ○Disagree ○Neutral/Mixed

24. My partner does not want to get as close as I would like.
○Agree ○Disagree ○Neutral/Mixed

25. I spend a great deal of time worrying about my relationship.
○Agree ○Disagree ○Neutral/Mixed

26. I prefer not to share my deep down feelings with my partner.
○Agree ○Disagree ○Neutral/Mixed

27. When not with my partner I worry he/she may be interested in someone else.
○Agree ○Disagree ○Neutral/Mixed

28. I often worry that my partner will leave me.
○Agree ○Disagree ○Neutral/Mixed

29. If my partner is not around when I need him/her, I get frustrated.
○Agree ○Disagree ○Neutral/Mixed

30. I worry that once my partner gets to know me he/she will no longer love me.
○Agree ○Disagree ○Neutral/Mixed

Review and Reflection

You've identified your attachment style. Now read its characteristics and consider these questions:

1. How well do you think the characteristics describe you?

_____

2. Is your style a blend of characteristics from more than one style?

_____

3. Does knowing your attachment style help you to better understand your feelings and behaviors?

_____

_____

4. Can you see any link between your family history and your attachment style?

_____

_____

5. Has this process helped you to "draw" the more intricate lines in your fingerprint?

_____

_____

Secure Attachment Style

◉ The ability to be warm and loving

◉ Comfortable with yourself and in your relationships

◉ Ability to be intimate without being overly worried

◉ Tendency to have happy, longer-lasting relationships

◉ Comfortable sharing feelings with your partner; ability to ask for support

◉ Not easily upset about relationship issues

◉ Communicates wants and needs effectively

◉ Good at responding to partner's cues

Anxious/Ambivalent Attachment Style

◉ Excessive worry about romantic relationships

◉ Worry that your feelings are not reciprocated

◉ Fear of abandonment

◉ Want to be close, but fear my partner may feel suffocated

◉ Great capacity for intimacy

◉ Relationships consume a majority of your emotional energy

◉ Sensitive to small fluctuations in partner's mood

◉ Easily upset

◉ Sometimes say things you later regret

Avoidant Attachment Style

◉ Independence and self-sufficiency are important

◉ Difficulty with close relationships

◉ Uncomfortable sharing thoughts, feelings, and ideas with a partner

◉ May come up with excuses to avoid intimacy

◉ Spend little time worrying about romantic relationships

◉ Partners may complain about emotional distance

◉ Vigilant about territory violations

Your attachment style can change over a lifetime, depending on your awareness and understanding of yourself. It always helps to have a little luck in romantic relationships and be paired with a partner whose attachment style is compatible with yours, or who feels empathy for the feelings and fears that come with your attachment style.

Erika and Andrew

To help you get a picture of the profound impact attachment styles can have on real people, a couple I saw a few years ago will serve to illustrate.

Andrew was the one to break the ice in our first session by saying, "I really hope you can help us. We're driving each other nuts. Our house is a constant battle zone, and neither one of us is happy. I think we're making our kids crazy too." Andrew was in his early thirties, with thick blond hair and blue eyes.

Erika, a tall African American woman, sat on the edge of her chair. "He gives nothing to our family. He claims that he's working all the time, but I don't believe him. He works with all of these young women. I think he's cheating on me. In fact, I know it, and it's making me sick. I worry about it day and night."

Andrew leapt from his chair. "That is just insane! I'm not cheating on you. Doctor, I work fifty to sixty hours a week as a software engineer. By the time I get home, I'm exhausted. If I'm too tired to make love, Erika thinks that means I'm cheating on her. It's ridiculous. Erika needs a reality check.

"I'll tell you something bizarre, Doctor. Erika and I have been together for nine years. We have two kids, a house, a dog, and a cat. The woman refuses to marry me. Just refuses."

Heatedly, Erika replied, "What's the point of marriage? You're going to leave me anyway. I'm just making it easier for you when you decide to go."

"We have this argument on a regular basis," Andrew said. "Erika is a jealous, possessive woman, but she won't marry me. I love her enormously and would do anything in the world for her, but whatever I do, it's never enough. It's so frustrating."

Erika, the only child of Haitian parents, had grown up in Florida. When Erika was six years old her father died of leukemia. Unable to support the two of them, her mother sent Erika to live with her aunt and uncle in New York. From the time of her arrival, they treated Erika like a servant. She was required to clean the house and baby-sit her cousins. During Erika's early adolescence, her uncle tried to sexually molest her on several occasions. Still, Erika's mother wouldn't let her return to Florida.

Andrew was a challenging choice for Erika. He had grown up the younger of two sons in a suburban setting. When Andrew was four, his older brother drowned in a neighbor's swimming pool. As a result, their mother became severely depressed. Andrew remembers his childhood as a flight from his family's grief.

Part of my work with Erika and Andrew involved helping them recognize that their attachment styles had developed in response to their life situations. Erika tended toward an anxious/ambivalent style, Andrew an avoidant style. Couples with this configuration of styles often have unstable relationships. The avoidant person's tendency is distancing, while the anxious partner fears abandonment.

Erika needed to understand that she viewed her relationship with Andrew through the lens of her attachment style. Their relationship was not in fact doomed. By developing an awareness of her inner workings, Erika gained some mastery of her emotions and came to accept that she was a person who might always be a little on the anxious side. She grew confident of her ability to handle her anxiety and not allow it to sabotage her relationships.

Andrew reluctantly examined his childhood lessons about relationships. He was able to confront his fear of loss, engulfment, and suffocation. Also, he dealt with the consequences of unresolved grief over the tragic death of his brother. By letting go of old baggage, Andrew was able to alter his behavior and become more available to Erika.

In this chapter you delved into your family history, learned about your behavior patterns and attachment style, and expanded your understanding of your inner relationship fingerprint. These are the building blocks of clarity about the nature of your relationships.

Chapter 6

The History of
Your Romantic Relationships

April and Bad Boys

April, a petite woman in her early thirties, took off a beret and shook her blonde hair as she entered my office. "Doc, you gotta help me," she began. "You'd think that I'd learn, but I just keep making the same mistake over and over again. I'm a moron.

"My boyfriend left me, again, like he's been doing for two years. He runs around, we argue, he leaves for a month or so, then calls me, tells me how much he misses me, and I take him back. I know I shouldn't." She shook her head and began to cry, "I just can't take it anymore. I'm worn out."

April worked as the office manager in a doctor's practice. She had been self-supporting since leaving home before she graduated from high school. She took pride in her responsibility and independence. Her problem was her weakness for guitar players.

"What can I tell you? Musicians are the only kind of guy that does it for me. I work around all sorts of professionals: doctors, male nurses, salespeople, and clients. Men hit on me all the time, but I'm not interested. I know I should hook up with a grown-up, responsible man, but somehow I just don't see it happening."

When I asked April to tell me what qualities attracted her to a man, she said, "I don't know. There's something about that 'bad-boy' type that appeals to me. The whole thing—jeans, long hair, tattoos, Fender guitar, Harley. Bad boys are free. They don't follow rules or care what anyone thinks. Pretty adolescent of me, huh?"

In the next few weeks, April shared her history. She told of her involvement in a series of relationships with unready or commitment-phobic men. April's parents divorced when she was eight. She and her younger brother grew up shuttling between houses. Her father, a college professor, had a history of affairs with his female students. Her mother, a social worker, ran an adoption agency.

April didn't remember spending much time as a child with her parents. As a result, she developed a precocious independence. Now she sees her parents only on holidays and birthdays. She talks to her brother, who lives in Alaska, every three years or so.

One day April said to me, "You know, Doc, I'm getting old—at least that's how I feel. I want to have a kid but I don't want to raise one myself, like some of my friends are doing. That looks too damn hard. I want to parent my kid with a partner. Is that too much to ask?"

"What would it mean for you to be in a committed relationship?"

"Part of it seems appealing, but in other ways kinda scary. I've been on my own, taking care of myself since before I can remember. I come and go as I please, and I don't have to answer to anybody. I can't handle anyone telling me what to do. My boyfriends haven't cared enough to bother. As long as I let them do their thing, I'm a free bird."

"So involvement in a committed relationship might mean giving up some your freedom?"

"I guess so. It's not like I'm some big rebel or wild child, but I wouldn't want someone thinking he can boss me around."

April was an intelligent, perceptive woman who was eager to change her modus operandi. Many young women go through a bad-boy stage for obvious and deep-seated reasons. Some love bad boys to compensate for their own need to be "good girls." A bad boy acts out a woman's unconscious desire for freedom from social rules and constraints. Most women outgrow this stage as they mature and seek more meaningful, stable relationships.

April's need for autonomy reinforced her attraction to men who wouldn't threaten her freedom. April saw her father as a bad boy, even though he was a professor. Men of this kind were familiar and comfortable for her. Her relationship with rebellious boyfriends allowed her to capture pieces of her father that she had missed during her childhood.

April's fingerprint reveals a highly independent individual. She watched her mother competently raise two children on her own. As an adult, unconsciously, April refused to emotionally invest in relationships. Her experience taught her that they don't last. April's early history became ingrained in her adult behavior.

In the next section, you'll have the opportunity to focus on your relationship history and identify patterns you might have as part of your inner relationship fingerprint.

A Visit to the Museum of Your Relationship History

Let's walk down memory lane and spend time with the ghosts of your past in the Museum of Your Relationship History. The purpose of delving into past relationships is to gather clues about your IRF. Like a good detective, you'll piece the clues together and form a cohesive explanation of motives and experiences. This kind of analysis sparks fresh insights and broadens perspective.

Be warned that parts of your tour may be sad or uncomfortable. Take a few deep breaths before you wipe the dust from the archives. Your reward for enduring any unpleasant emotions will be a deeper awareness and understanding of your inner workings, which you know is the first step toward transformation. As Winston Churchill said, "Those who fail to learn from history are doomed to repeat it."

Ready to begin? Start with your most current partner. Use a separate sheet of paper if you run out of space.

Significant Relationship Number I

1. What attracted you to this person?

_____

_____

_____

2. If the relationship ended, how long did it last?

_____

3. What did/do you like most about this person?

_____

_____

_____

4. What did/do you like least about this person?

_____

_____

_____

5. What role did you play in relationship? (To stimulate your thinking about possible roles, see the chart below.)

_____

_____

_____

Chart of Relationship Roles

nurturer	*joker*	*rebel*	*rule-keeper*
caretaker	*worrier*	*child*	*friend*
mother	*martyr*	*protector*	*submissive*
ambivalent	*victim*	*rescuer/rescued*	*self-pitying*
teacher	*father*	*seducer*	*dominant*
breadwinner	*high-roller*	*bad boy*	*hero*

6. What role(s) did your partner play?

_____

_____

7. How did you feel in the relationship (i.e., loved, suffocated, overwhelmed, sexual, anxious, safe, dependent, ambivalent, in dread, etc.)?

_____

_____

8. If there are/were problems in the relationship, what were/are they (sex, money, anger, control, unfinished business, nagging, guilt, step-children, parenting skills, etc.)?

_____

_____

9. If the relationship ended, why and how did it end? At what point did you know the relationship wasn't going to work or that your needs were not satisfied?

_____

_____

10. If the relationship ended, how did you feel about it ending (i.e., sad, relieved, ambivalent, happy, guilty)?

_____

_____

_____

Significant Relationship Number 2

1. What attracted you to this person?

_____

_____

_____

2. If the relationship ended, how long did it last?

_____

3. What did/do you like most about this person?

_____

_____

_____

4. What did/do you like least about this person?

_____

_____

_____

5. What role did you play in relationship? (To stimulate your thinking about possible roles, see the chart below.)

_____

_____

_____

Chart of Relationship Roles

nurturer	joker	rebel	rule-keeper
caretaker	worrier	child	friend
mother	martyr	protector	submissive
ambivalent	victim	rescuer/rescued	self-pitying
teacher	father	seducer	dominant
breadwinner	high-roller	bad boy	hero

6. What role(s) did your partner play?

_____

_____

7. How did you feel in the relationship (i.e., loved, suffocated, overwhelmed, sexual, anxious, safe, dependent, ambivalent, in dread, etc.)?

_____

_____

8. If there are/were problems in the relationship, what were/are they (sex, money, anger, control, unfinished business, nagging, guilt, step-children, parenting skills, etc.)?

_____

_____

9. If the relationship ended, why and how did it end? At what point did you know the relationship wasn't going to work or that your needs were not satisfied?

_____

_____

_____

10. If the relationship ended, how did you feel about it ending (i.e., sad, relieved, ambivalent, happy, guilty)?

_____

_____

_____

Significant Relationship Number 3

1. What attracted you to this person?

_____

_____

2. If the relationship ended, how long did it last?

_____

3. What did/do you like most about this person?

_____

_____

_____

4. What did/do you like least about this person?

_____

_____

_____

5. What role did you play in relationship? (To stimulate your thinking about possible roles, see the chart below.)

_____

_____

Chart of Relationship Roles

nurturer	*joker*	*rebel*	*rule-keeper*
caretaker	*worrier*	*child*	*friend*
mother	*martyr*	*protector*	*submissive*
ambivalent	*victim*	*rescuer/rescued*	*self-pitying*
teacher	*father*	*seducer*	*dominant*
breadwinner	*high-roller*	*bad boy*	*hero*

6. What role(s) did your partner play?

_____

_____

7. How did you feel in the relationship (i.e., loved, suffocated, overwhelmed, sexual, anxious, safe, dependent, ambivalent, dread, etc.)?

_____

_____

8. If there are/were problems in the relationship, what were/are they (sex, money, anger, control, unfinished business, nagging, guilt, step-children, parenting skills, etc.)?

_____

_____

_____

9. If the relationship ended, why and how did it end? At what point did you know the relationship wasn't going to work or that your needs were not satisfied?

---

10. If the relationship ended, how did you feel about ending (i.e., sad, relieved, ambivalent, happy, guilty)?

Review and Reflection — Museum Visit

How did it go? Did you have a pleasant trip down memory lane? Or was it the reunion from hell? Put on your detective's hat to organize and then analyze your findings. The questions below will help you.

List any similarities you found in what initially attracted you to partners.

List any differences you found in what initially attracted you to partners.

If you see any patterns in your initial attractions, list them.

_____

_____

_____

Did you find that your role(s) tended to be similar in each relationship?

_____

_____

_____

Were there similarities about the way the relationships ended? What are your thoughts about those endings?

_____

_____

_____

6. What was your subjective experience while touring the Museum of Relationship History (i.e., a sense of foreboding, dread, guilt, despair, relief, freedom)?

_____

_____

_____

A Word about Patterns

Patterns in relationships are part of your inner relationship fingerprint. Each unconscious pattern replays over and over, deepening the grooves in your neural pathways. This is why breaking patterns challenges even the most persistent among us.

For example, a person with "nurturer" burned into his or her fingerprint will tend to be the nurturer in all relationships.

Someone who carries the victim trait will find ways to be victimized repeatedly. A rebel will find the constraints of relationships difficult. A hero seeks people to rescue.

People repeat the same relationship patterns. The IRF exerts a force as powerful as gravity, which makes it difficult, but not impossible, to change. Consider your own choices in partners. Do you seek someone just like you, or a person who possesses certain qualities you wish you had? If you are shy, you might be drawn to someone who's outgoing. If you're an only child, you might be attracted to someone with a big, happy family. Many people try unconsciously to recreate the dynamics of their parents' relationship, no matter how unhappy, unhealthy, or tumultuous.

Simply put, if you want to break a particular pattern, you first need to understand it from your inside out. Get familiar with the pattern—where it came from and how you express it in relationships with your partner, friends, boss, and coworkers.

For April to break out of her bad-boy pattern, she needed first to identify its origins and expression. Once she recognized what she was doing and why, she weaned herself from rock stars and slowly began to spend time with men more likely to satisfy her adult needs and wants.

April didn't believe that love could last, so she sought men whose behavior reaffirmed this core belief. She isn't alone. Everyone is attracted to relationships that confirm their core beliefs about love and life. Core beliefs are rooted in our inner relationship fingerprint. Only by becoming fully aware of these beliefs and patterns can you begin to make choices that change the flow of your history.

Chapter 7

Self-Expectations — Are You Your Own Worst Enemy?

Recently, my wife, Meg, and I were invited to dinner at the home of our friends Paula and Steve — a couple married for over twenty years. The atmosphere of their house is warm and comfortable, a mirror of their relationship.

As the four of us lingered over dessert, we talked about whether we choose our roles in life or our roles choose us. Paula, a feminist and successful professional, told us that as a wife she believed it was her responsibility to cook meals for Steve.

A surprised Steve told us he had never expected Paula to be the cook, and added that he loved and appreciated Paula's cooking, but in truth he preferred to eat in restaurants. With some reluctance, he had given up eating out so as to accommodate Paula's passion for cooking. Needless to say, Paula was shocked.

Paula had never examined her own assumptions about what it meant to be a wife. Her IRF wrote the script: marriage came with implicit roles and responsibilities. Paula realized that she derived pleasure from serving homemade meals, and was doing it for herself as much as for Steve.

What Do You Expect From Yourself?

Your expectations of yourself propel you forward or hold you back. They influence your thoughts, feelings, and experiences in the world. I'm not talking about what your family or friends expect, although it's true that your expectations are rooted in your fingerprint. I'm talking about what *you* expect from yourself. People have both positive and negative expectations of themselves. Some expectations are realistic while others are unrealistic. You might wonder where your expectations came from. It's hard to differentiate whether they originated from within you or from your external environment (family, friends, society, media, books, etc.).

Since birth you have heard messages that shaped your self-perception and thus your expectations of yourself. Parents both praise and criticize their children. Some parents are predominantly critical; others do nothing but praise, and some dole out a balanced amount of praise and criticism.

Negative messages can make a person feel inferior. Children internalize labels like lazy, irresponsible, sloppy, stupid, clumsy, ugly, etc. They take their parents' words to heart. As a fifth grader struggling to learn long division, I had the same teacher who, several years before, had taught my high-achiever sister. I will never forget the teacher asking me, "Are you really Neela's brother?" Her comment made me believe that I really was a dimwit.

Have your self-expectations squeezed you into a small box? Do you ever have thoughts like: *I am not rich enough, not smart enough, not fit enough, not enough enough?* Do you expect all of these things and feel that you don't measure up? Let me give you an example. When was the last time you decided *not* to try something new, like Tai Chi, pool, watercolors, cliff diving, pole dancing, or Angry Birds? Did you predict that you wouldn't be good at it? Are you reluctant to try new things because you fear that you'll fail? Do you attribute your failure to your own negative expectations?

Expectations can be self-fulfilling prophecies. If you believe that you'll be good at a new activity, then it's more likely you'll be good — and vice-versa: Think failure, and the likelihood of failure increases; expect success, and chances are good things will go your way. The power of positive thinking is all about your expectations at the outset.

Honestly, what's stated in the previous paragraph is *sometimes* true. Positive expectations do not guarantee success. As a young boy, I fully believed that I would play Major League Baseball. My expectation was solely my own fantasy; it was never encouraged by my family, teachers, or coaches, and it didn't happen. I just didn't have the athletic ability. There are many reasons why your expectations can go unfulfilled. Sometimes they're unrealistic, like my baseball fantasy. Have there been times in your life when your visions for yourself didn't materialize? Sometimes a particular opportunity is just not available. Life can be hard that way.

What Do You Expect From **Yourself** in Relationships?

In relationships your self-expectations can be positive or negative, realistic or unrealistic, and conscious or unconscious. They are woven into your IRF. Your expectations guide your actions, reactions, and decisions.

The next exercise shines a light on characteristics we commonly expect of one another in relationships. Your task is to identify the characteristics *you* expect of yourself in your relationship. Check the ones that resonate with you. And, of course, feel free to add others. Make selections from the list for either gender — the gender designations are for convenience, and are not intended to create barriers or be stereotypical.

Men's Self-Expectations

❑ Good provider

❑ Protector

❑ Attentive to partner

❑ Intelligent/knowledgeable/interesting

❑ Contributes financially

❑ Problem solver

❑ Good father

❑ Sexually attractive to partner

❑ Able to sexually satisfy partner

❑ Handy around the house

❑ Honest and trustworthy

❑ Dependable

❑ Good companion

❑ Faithful

❑ Entertaining

❑ Other _____

❑ Other _____

Women's Self-Expectations

- ❑ Intelligent, well informed
- ❑ Good mother
- ❑ Homemaker
- ❑ Good conversationalist
- ❑ Contributes financially
- ❑ Faithful
- ❑ Good listener
- ❑ Good companion
- ❑ Honest, trustworthy
- ❑ Inspiring
- ❑ Nurturing
- ❑ Understanding/Empathic
- ❑ Best friend
- ❑ Breadwinner
- ❑ Affectionate
- ❑ Sexually attractive to partner
- ❑ Superwoman
- ❑ Other_____
- ❑ Other_____

Review and Reflection — Self-Expectations

1. Count the number of roles and traits you marked. How many did you check?

_____

2. How would you rate your expectations of yourself (high, medium, low)?

_____

3. Which of your expectations are realistic? Which are unrealistic?

_____

_____

_____

4. Which roles/traits do you like?

_____

_____

_____

5. Which roles/traits do you resent? Did you consciously choose them?

_____

_____

_____

6. Are there roles/traits you find difficult?

_____

_____

_____

7. Are there any roles you would be relieved to give up? Is it possible to relinquish any of these roles?

_____

_____

_____

8. Who might resist your giving up a role?

_____

_____

_____

Do Your Self-Expectations Really Belong to You?

Okay, now it's time to sort through all your self-expectations and identify their sources. Did these expectations originate with you or with your family, partner, or children? It might be difficult to trace your self-expectations back to their origins. Use the guidelines below to help you explore them:

◙ Your potential;

◙ Your ability (intellectual, athletic, artistic, technical, etc.);

◙ Your strengths and deficits;

◙ Your opportunities (education, luck, social status, role models, parentage, etc.);

◙ Your values (freedom, love, connection, money, education, etc.);

◙ Your aspirations (to be president, 21st-century Buddha, a billionaire, Tom Brady, Lady Gaga, Mother Theresa, Jon Stewart, Hilary Clinton, etc.);

◎ Your fears (ridicule, shame, embarrassment, failure, abandonment, criticism, etc.);

◎ Your character traits (persevering, hardworking, manipulative, lazy, empathic, loyal, brave, etc.);

◎ Your experiences (successes, failures, relationships, adventures, travel, role models, etc.);

◎ Your desires (fame, fortune, family, peace, attention, excitement, tranquility, etc.).

In this exercise you explored your expectations of yourself. You probably noticed that some of the listed items have helped you reaching your potential while others have hindered you from reaching it. Being clear about your expectations of yourself is important. Often when people feel pressured, overwhelmed, or unhappy about some aspect of life, they blame their partners. They may resent feeling coerced to fulfill a specific role based on their partners' expectations, when in reality the expectations are coming from themselves or deeply embedded in their IRF.

To illustrate: Don feels driven to earn large sums of money. When the pressure in his business builds, he often blames his wife for expecting a high standard of living. In reality, his wife would prefer he spend more time at home. Don's demand for high income is self-imposed and derives from his childhood experience of poverty.

The point: We need to own our expectations of ourselves and be careful not to attribute them to others. Getting clear on your expectations will get you on track to realistic, reachable goals that you have set intentionally based on your own needs and wants.

Chapter 8

Do Your Wants and Needs
Align with Your Actual Life?

Glenda and Charlene Adjust
to Unfamiliar Roles

Glenda and Charlene showed up ten minutes late for their appointment. Both looked frazzled. I interviewed them separately to give each an opportunity to talk to me privately. Charlene offered to go first.

Charlene, then in her early forties, was tall, thin, and smartly dressed. She earned a six-figure salary as a human resource director for a Fortune 500 company. I didn't have to be Sigmund Freud to realize she was a frustrated woman. It took only a few gentle questions to peel away Charlene's cool exterior and reveal a woman in deep pain. Between sobs she told me that her marriage had failed, that she had failed. She no longer loved Glenda; she was not the woman she thought she had committed to for life.

Glenda, a patent lawyer, had been a young rising associate at a high-powered firm. Three years before, the firm had informed Glenda that she would not be considered for partnership. Glenda was so hurt and angry that she left the firm immediately and refused to seek another position. Instead, by default, she became a stay-at-home mom.

"I could deal with Glenda being Suzy Homemaker Mom if she weren't so bitter and resentful," Charlene said. "Evenings when I get home, she barely talks to me and never asks about my day. She yells at our boys, who are five and seven. She doesn't seem to care about me at all. I feel like I'm nothing but a paycheck to her. Even though I make all the money, she complains when I buy work clothes, and she refuses to eat out—she won't pay for a babysitter.

"And to make matters worse, she refuses to have sex with me. She says she's too tired after being with the kids all day. We haven't had sex for eight months. She doesn't even want to touch me. I think she finds me repulsive. When I try to talk to her, she won't talk about what's going on for her. She completely shuts me out. This isn't the duty I signed up for. I agreed to counseling for my sons' sake. I want them to grow up with both of us, but frankly I'm not sure I can spend another day with this angry woman."

Glenda was next. She was slender and of average height, with curly brown hair. Her eyes revealed an intensity that made me a little uncomfortable. They grew almost fierce as she raged about her "self-centered, selfish, superficial partner."

"Doc, do you know what a bitch Charlene is? In the morning she spends so much time in the mirror, she doesn't even acknowledge the kids, let alone think about giving them breakfast. And dinner... forget dinner, she hasn't had dinner with the kids and me for months! I'm making a big career sacrifice so one of us is home with the kids. I do all the schlepping and all the housework, and get nothing in return. She completely ignores me. She never really understood the pain I went through after the firm dumped me. Since I started taking Paxil for depression, I have no interest in sex. But really, that's okay. I don't miss it.

No sex is better than having sex with a selfish bitch."

When I commented that she seemed angry, Glenda said, "Angry? You bet I'm angry!"

Our initial work focused on Charlene and Glenda's individual anger about their situation. We would deal with their anger at each other later. We explored the uncomfortable roles that they were surprised to have found themselves mired in. Charlene resented being the breadwinner, and Glenda had never aspired to being a full-time homemaker. It turned out that their anger was less at each other than about the roles that their circumstances had placed them in.

> After only a few sessions it dawned on Glenda that her anger at Charlene was misdirected; she felt angry and disappointed with herself for her failure to make partner. Instead of owning her feelings about abandoning her career, Glenda took out her rage on Charlene. Glenda recognized that she wanted to go back to work. She needed the intellectual stimulation her profession provides. She missed the satisfaction of earning money. She decided that, rather than returning to the world of high-powered law, she would open her own practice.
>
> Charlene admitted that for a long time she resented being the sole breadwinner. She acknowledged that she had been unavailable to Glenda and the boys. She wanted a deeper connection with Glenda and a greater involvement with the family.

What Do You Want?

What do you need? What do you want? You'd think these wouldn't be tough questions, but let me tell you, it turns out they're tough. When I ask them of my clients, they often respond with a blank stare, followed by a weak "I don't really know," their voices trailing off at the end. Sometimes I feel like a waiter asking people to place their orders without giving them a menu. After a moment's reflection, some might add:

"I want him to listen to me."

"I need to have sex more often"

"I wish he made more money"

"I want her to watch sports with me."

When we were children, our parents programmed us. They told us what to do, think, and feel: eat your spinach; now it's bedtime; Aunt Tillie is nice; be polite; don't be angry. If only it had stopped with parents. Teachers told us how to think. Now, bosses tell us to work harder. Ministers tell us how to pray. Friends tell us how to play. Our families tell us all the rest. We're bombarded every day with 10,000 advertisements and brand impressions telling us what to do, be, and buy or we won't be happy. All this noise makes it difficult to know what's right for us — it's no wonder that people don't have ready answers.

If you're like my clients, you could use clarity about your needs and wants. First, let's create a framework for analysis so we can get straight about the difference between a need and a want. A *need* is something you *must* have. Your survival might depend on it. A need has no room for negotiation. Suppression or denial of a need will take a toll on you. For example, I need to be respected by my partner, to eat three meals a day, and to feel secure in my relationship.

A *want* is something you would *like to* have, a preference, or a desire. It enhances your life, but you could live without it. For example, I want a vacation in Italy, a new set of golf clubs, and a wife who is a magician.

To stimulate your thinking, review the following list of needs and wants. The list is not intended to be comprehensive, so personalize it by adding your own needs and wants.

Safety Needs and Wants

To know that your partner is committed to the relationship;

To know that your partner will stand by you in crisis/time of distress;

To be confident that your partner will rally to your aid if needed;

To feel your partner's unquestionable loyalty;

To know your partner won't intentionally hurt you emotionally or physically.

Physical Needs and Wants

To be touched;

To be hugged;

Physical tenderness;

To have a satisfying sexual life;

To live in a peaceful, harmonious environment.

Spiritual Needs and Wants

To have similar spiritual beliefs.

The freedom to have different spiritual beliefs;

To feel supported in your spiritual beliefs.

Emotional Needs and Wants

To feel loved;

To feel cared for by your partner;

To be respected by your partner;

To be desired by your partner;

To be special to your partner;

To be known by your partner.

Now that you've had an opportunity to inventory your needs and wants, let's get more specific and explore what you need and want in a partner.

Exercise: What Traits Does
Your Ideal Partner Possess?

If you could create the perfect partner, what traits would he or she possess? What do you absolutely need and cannot be without? What do you *want,* but could live without? What wants or needs don't matter to you?

The tables below (one for men, one for women) contain a comprehensive menu of traits. Carefully read through the menu, and decide for each item whether the trait is one that you need or want in a partner or that you feel is unimportant. As you do the exercise, stay focused on what you want and need. Let go of judgment, and avoid the tendency to think only in terms of your current partner. Be honest. One answer is not better than another. Mark your wants and needs even if you know your partner lacks that particular trait. This exercise is about *you* and not your partner. Dream a little. Have some fun.

CREATE THE PROFILE OF YOUR IDEAL PARTNER
(MEN'S LIST)

TRAIT	WANT	NEED	NOT IMPORTANT
A friend			
A good girl/boy			
A good-time gal/guy who's focused on me			
Abstains from alcohol/drugs			
Adventurous			
Attractive			
Brave			
Career-minded			
Charming			
Compassionate			
Doesn't embarrass me			
Doesn't make me feel guilty			
Doesn't make more money than I do			
Doesn't over-indulge in alcohol/drugs			
Doesn't whine			
Easy to talk to/good communicator			
Faithful			
Fun			
Good cook			
Good mother			
Healthy habits			

Trait	Want	Need	Not Important
Helps with housework			
Honest			
Humorous			
Independent			
Intelligent			
Introspective			
Involved in community/volunteers			
Kinky			
Lets me be dominant			
Likes oral sex			
Likes and wants children			
Not prone to temper tantrums/angry outbursts			
Not too aggressive			
Not too needy			
Nurturing			
Open and honest			
Optimistic			
Passive			
Persevering			
Playful			
Practical			
Religious/Spiritual			
Risk taker			

TRAIT	WANT	NEED	NOT IMPORTANT
Romantic			
Same worldview			
Sexy			
Shares my political persuasion			
Shares similar taste in music/movies			
Not flirtatious			
Someone I can possess			
Stylish, well-groomed			
Supportive			
Takes care of his/her health			
Talkative			
Talks dirty			
Talks politics			
Tells me what he/she wants			
Tidy			
Tolerates my idiosyncrasies/quirks			
Treats me respectfully			
Trustworthy			
Validates my needs			
Voluptuous body			
Willing to watch sports with me			
Worldly, sophisticated			
Other			

CREATE A PROFILE OF YOUR IDEAL PARTNER
(WOMEN'S LIST)

TRAIT	WANT	NEED	NOT IMPORTANT
A friend			
A good girl/boy			
A good-time gal/guy who's focused on me			
Abstains from alcohol/drugs			
Adventurous			
Attractive			
Brave			
Career-minded			
Charming			
Compassionate			
Doesn't embarrass me			
Doesn't make me feel guilty			
Doesn't make more money than I do			
Doesn't over-indulge in alcohol/drugs			
Doesn't whine			
Easy to talk to/good communicator			
Faithful			
Fun			
Good cook			
Good mother			
Healthy habits			

Trait	Want	Need	Not Important
Helps with housework			
Honest			
Humorous			
Independent			
Intelligent			
Introspective			
Involved in community/volunteers			
Kinky			
Lets me be dominant			
Likes oral sex			
Likes and wants children			
Not prone to temper tantrums/angry outbursts			
Not too aggressive			
Not too needy			
Nurturing			
Open and honest			
Optimistic			
Passive			
Persevering			
Playful			
Practical			
Religious/Spiritual			
Risk taker			

Trait	Want	Need	Not Important
Romantic			
Same worldview			
Sexy			
Shares my political persuasion			
Shares similar taste in music/movies			
Not flirtatious			
Someone I can possess			
Stylish, well-groomed			
Supportive			
Takes care of his/her health			
Talkative			
Talks dirty			
Talks politics			
Tells me what he/she wants			
Tidy			
Tolerates my idiosyncrasies/quirks			
Treats me respectfully			
Trustworthy			
Validates my needs			
Voluptuous body			
Willing to watch sports with me			
Worldly, sophisticated			
Other			

Review your responses. Choose your top ten needs and top ten wants and list them below. Then do your best to prioritize your needs and wants according to their relative importance.

My Top Ten Needs

1. _____
2. _____
3. _____
4. _____
5. _____
6. _____
7. _____
8. _____
9. _____
10. _____

My Top Ten Wants

1. _____
2. _____
3. _____
4. _____
5. _____
6. _____
7. _____
8. _____
9. _____
10. _____

Review and Reflection — Ideal Partner Traits

What is your impression of the lists you compiled?

_____

_____

_____

Are your lists indicative of who you really are? Do they reflect your values and beliefs?

_____

_____

Does your partner meet any of your top ten needs? Which ones?

_____

_____

Does your partner meet any of your top ten wants? Which ones?

_____

_____

_____

Name your needs that your partner does not satisfy.

_____

_____

_____

Name your wants that your partner does not satisfy.

_____

_____

_____

7. Would it be possible for your partner to acquire traits that you need or want that he or she lacks (i.e., while he or she can't grow long legs, could he or she learn to be more empathic)?

_____

_____

_____

8. How important are changes to you? How would life be different? How would you feel?

_____

_____

_____

In this chapter you discovered which of your needs and wants are most important to you. This new clarity puts you in a position to see your relationship in perspective. If there are gaps between your needs/wants and your relationship, don't worry — part 2 gives you strategies to help bridge the gap. But first, let's review your progress in part 1.

Chapter 9

Review and Reflection —
Celebrate Your Progress

Congratulations on reaching a hard-won milestone. You have completed Part 1 of *Relationship Transformation*. On this leg of your journey, you've become expert in self-focus. You've tuned up your self-awareness to prepare the foundation for a healthier, more satisfying relationship. If you're like most people, the road to self-awareness wasn't easy. It might have been surprising. Did you discover new aspects of yourself? Did you find them humorous, embarrassing, uncomfortable, or shameful? What discovery made you feel proud?

Let's take time to review your work. Don't worry—you won't be graded. Remember the guidelines: Keep the focus on you. Stay in the judgment-free zone. Be kind to yourself. In your exploration, you no doubt found a human being with a history of hurts, joys, failures, hopes, and dreams. In you, there is a person who is trying his or her best to play the hand that life has dealt you.

1. Freedom-Security Styles. Were you able to identify your freedom-security style? Did this exploration lead to any new insights? Do you feel the need to rebalance the competing needs of freedom and security in your relationship? Would creating a space for freedom add a little zing, or do you seek greater security?

2. The WYOU Exercise. Did your ability to tune in improve over time? Were you the first person who could tune in to all 50,000 thoughts? Were any messages repetitive? How do you feel about the broadcast?

3. Still-Point Meditation. How did you feel about the Still-Point Meditation? Did you incorporate the practice into your daily life? Did it bring clarity? In what way? Did it change your mood or level of anxiety? Were there other benefits?

4. The Museum of Relationship History Exercise. Did you identify any patterns in your relationship history? What were the similarities in your choices of partners, roles, or experiences?

5. Needs and Wants. You identified your ideal partner. Did your wants and needs surprise you? Did you have difficulty prioritizing them? How does your current partner match your lists of wants and needs? Did you discover any major gaps?

6. The Inner Relationship Fingerprint. Does your IRF accurately reflect your personality? Did your exploration lead to any insights? Do you feel that it deepened your understanding of yourself? Did you have any life-changing epiphanies?

In part 2 you will use your newly clarified perspective to evaluate your situation and plot a course for a more satisfying connection with your partner. Are you ready to create your compelling relationship vision?

Chapter 10

Create Your Compelling Relationship Vision

Simone and Tom Work to Align Differing Visions

As Simone and Tom entered my office, they struck me as a defeated pair. In their late thirties, both were well dressed and immaculately groomed. Simone said, "Doctor, I'm afraid we might be wasting your time. We're beyond help. I don't think there's anything anyone can do."

I asked them to tell me what was happening in their relationship. Tom answered first: "To tell you the truth, I'm surprised to be here. No offense, but I've always believed therapy was for losers and whiners. Then, when Simone told me that she and her attorney were ready to file for divorce, I didn't know what else to do. I'm like a dying atheist who suddenly believes in God. I'm desperate to save our marriage."

Simone and Tom shared the story of their life together. They met as students at an Ivy League college. Tom was the eldest of three children from a working-class background. His father was an electrician, his mother a dental receptionist. From an early age, Tom was serious, exceedingly bright, and ambitious. When he met Simone, he was a senior on full scholarship and getting ready to graduate.

Simone had never spent time with someone from Tom's background and with his earnestness. Most of her playmates were young men from wealthy families who knew more about beer than Baudelaire. She had come within an eyelash of flunking out after a freshman year of partying and debauchery.

Never a serious student, Simone had gained admittance to the prestigious school due only to the legacy of her father and grandfather. The youngest of five children, three of whom had attended the school before her, Simone was following in the family tradition — except that she was the "wild child" of the family.

Simone met Tom when she needed to get help in math and statistics to avoid getting thrown out of college. As it turned out, Tom was a tutor as part of his scholarship program, and took on Simone as a student. She found him a refreshing change from the men she knew, respected his sincerity and determination, and envied his having an actual plan for his future.

One night after a lesson, Tom ended up in Simone's bed. During this phase, Simone had multiple sex partners and didn't use birth control. Instead of having another abortion, she opted to have the baby. Simone hoped that by marrying someone like Tom, her life might get straightened out. She told Tom he was the father, and insisted they marry. For his part, Tom was elated to marry Simone, a woman he saw as out of his league. Simone never told Tom that the child might not be his.

Tom graduated with an engineering degree and went to work for a large corporation. He moved quickly into a lucrative managerial position with international responsibilities. Simone left college to take care of their daughter and become a homemaker.

Over the next fifteen years, Tom and Simone added two more

children, two dogs, and three cats. They lived north of Boston, on an estate near the ocean. Tom's business took him to Asia for weeks at a time. Simone didn't mind his being away, but she found the transitions when he came home difficult. She described their relationship as "cordial," without anger or argument.

Tom and Simone knew about each other's infidelities. Simone had been the first to break the ice eight years before, when she had an affair with her personal trainer. When Tom found out, he told Simone that he knew, but rationalized that she was probably lonely while he was gone. Tom was not one for emotional outbursts; however, he then began to visit prostitutes in Asia. Neither Tom nor Simone made any effort to hide their infidelities. Periodically, they would acknowledge them in passing, as if discussing the weather.

I asked Simone, "What do you want?"

She answered, "I don't know, but I don't want this." Beneath the façade of a perfect couple lived two people in despair. They were lonely and alienated, and didn't know what they wanted from each other.

Dealing with the Gaps

When you look carefully at your life, you will no doubt discover things about yourself that you wish were different. You wouldn't be human if you didn't. You might wish that you had more money, more knowledge, more talent, a different job, a newer car, a better disposition, or more time to spend with your family. Maybe the gap for you relates to your relationship. You might wish that your partner was more sensitive to your needs, more passionate, taller, thinner, or sexier. Perhaps you wish you had more help with the housework, more respect, fewer demands, less arguing, more reciprocity, or more/less sex. There's always something—dissatisfaction is part of our DNA.

When I suggest to clients that they close some of the gaps between what they have and what they want, they often respond with some version of either "No, it's not possible" or "I'm just being ungrateful, I should be more accepting." These answers reveal their beliefs about change, their feelings about self-worth, and their low expectations regarding relationship satisfaction.

Is it wrong to want something better than you have now? This question gnawed at Simone. On one level, she had everything anyone could want: a successful husband, beautiful houses, healthy children, and more money than she could spend. She felt she wasn't entitled to want something more or different, so she never bothered to identify her needs. Simone knew only what she didn't want, and was unhappy to the point of harboring suicidal fantasies.

To deal with the gaps you need to know yourself. I mean *really* know yourself. You need to be clear about your own priorities, and identify what is essentially important and what matters less. In part 1, you explored your core beliefs and your inner relationship fingerprint. From this heightened perspective you identified your most significant needs and wants with regard to your relationship.

Given what you've learned about yourself, would it be wrong to want some changes? One of the steps in the process of change involves measuring the size of the gap between what you want and what you have in your relationship. Are we talking the Grand Canyon or a narrow ravine?

I understand that any departure from the status quo can feel scary. Many of us believe the devil we know is better than the devil we don't. Why risk making a situation worse? Well, if you agree with the Dalai Lama that our purpose in life is happiness on this earth, your desire for joy — to have your cake and eat it too — will fuel your courage to take the risk.

Measuring the Gap

Here's an exercise to help you. Before you begin, consider going to your still point—the place where truth and clarity reside—and then return to this exercise. When you're ready, use the prompts and fill in the blanks with the first response that comes to your mind. Don't be tempted by the tendency to over-think. Once you've completed the blanks, go back and decide whether what you've identified is a want or a need, and circle the accurate label.

1. My relationship is _____

I need/want it to be _____

2. My relationship is _____

I need/want it to be _____

3. My relationship is _____

I need/want it to be _____

4. The predominant feeling I have when I look into my partner's eyes is _____

I need/want it to be _____

5. My partner is _____

I need/want him/her to be _____

6. My partner is _____

I need/want him/her to be _____

7. My partner is _____

I need/want him/her to be _____

8. My partner is _____

I need/want him/her to be _____

9. My life is _____

I need/want it to be _____

10. My life is _____

I need/want it to be _____

Review and Reflection: What feelings or thoughts do your responses evoke? Can the gap between your current reality and your needs and wants be narrowed by small corrections or redirection? Is the divide a huge canyon that seems insurmountable? At the moment, you are just measuring of the gaps. As you proceed through the next sections, you'll have the opportunity to concentrate on bridging the divide. Don't worry — I've got your back.

Creating Your Compelling Relationship Vision

Are you ready to re-envision your relationship? To break through unnecessary boundaries? To expand your notions of the possibilities of life with your partner? The visioning process creates clarity, builds confidence, and energizes you with laser-like focus. Have faith — unique and creative solutions will materialize as you move ahead.

How to Create a Vivid and Refreshing Vision

Your goal is to create a detailed and alluring mental picture of your ideal relationship. Don't limit your vision in any way. Go for it. Don't choke your fantasy with negative thoughts that arise, such as: *Whom are you trying to kid? Right, that would work with five kids. No way, never happen. Why bother?* Let the negative thoughts float by without catching hold of them.

You know all about those self-defeating negative voices that swirl around in your brain. It's time to tune them out. Remember, it's your vision, and you can have it any way you want. Make it extra-pleasurable. If it helps envision cakes—devil's food, red velvet, angel food, towering seven layer, orange-glow chiffon cake, cupcakes. Cake evokes sweetness, happiness, fun, and celebration. Taste, smell, see, and feel these emotions spread throughout your body. What's there to lose?

Now for some pointers to make your vision as vivid and refreshing as you possibly can:

◉ Be open to dramatic changes.

◉ Create vivid images.

◉ Bathe in the positive emotions your vision evokes.

◉ Draw on your beliefs and values.

◉ Do not assume any particular framework or style.

◉ Luxuriate in all your senses.

◉ Be positive and loving.

◉ Be confident.

◉ Feel inspired.

◉ Relax.

Liftoff: To start, use the still-point meditation to quiet your mind and access your deepest self. From your still point, imagine your ideal life with your ideal partner. Incorporate all your senses and emotions. Feel in your body what it's like to live your vision.

Take your time. Let your imagination take you where it wants to go. I'll be here when you return — with a piece of chocolate-raspberry ganache cake if you'd like.

Review and Reflection —
Your Relationship Vision

Welcome back. Take a few minutes to jot down your impressions of your vision. Use these questions as a guide:

1. What feelings did your vision evoke?

_____

_____

_____

2. How does the relationship in your vision differ from your relationship in reality?

_____

_____

_____

3. In what ways, if any, are *you* different in your vision?

_____

_____

_____

4. In what ways is your envisioned partner different from your actual partner?

_____

_____

_____

5. Can you brainstorm ways to bridge the gap between your vision and reality?

_____

_____

_____

Simone and Tom Unveil Their Relationship Visions

In my work with Simone and Tom, I asked each of them to create a separate relationship vision. Simone's vision of her life was nothing like her current life. In her vision, she was free and unencumbered. She traveled, met creative, artistic people, worked at something she loved, had exotic lovers, and spent her time gallivanting around a city.

In reality, she had never aspired to be a full-time homemaker and mother, let alone with a husband away on business. She felt tied down and lonely. She had never identified her needs or wants or explored her IRF, and she was unaware of the power it exerted in her life. She didn't realize that her fingerprint left her poorly equipped for full-time motherhood and homemaking. Although she loved Tom and her children, their marriage would require major renovation to survive.

Tom's vision centered around making Simone happy and keeping his family together. He told me he didn't want to lose Simone and could not envision life without her. He was willing to make whatever changes were necessary, even if that meant quitting his job.

Obviously, Tom and Simone had a number of issues to resolve — the demands of his business, their histories of infidelity, mistrust, and deception. After a few meetings it became clear that they were both invested in continuing to be together — always a good sign. Tom and Simone got creative and brainstormed new ways of living that would better meet their needs. They were ready to reclaim their marriage.

Simone's vision led her to realize that she needed a life of her own, outside her roles as wife and mother. She also wanted a deeper, more intimate connection with Tom. Tom kept his job. The family moved to Hong Kong, home of his corporate headquarters. To their credit, Tom and Simone decided to wipe the slate clean and begin their partnership anew. They let go of the past and grew excited about their new life together.

Simone acknowledged that vestiges of the "wild child" still lived in her, but now she'd try to channel that energy productively. Once she was settled in her new home, she opened an art gallery in Hong Kong. There she met creative people, accepted invitations to swanky cocktail parties, and discovered the city's artistic treasures.

To transform their lives was easier than either Simone or Tom had ever imagined. And you'll find it easier than you imagine too. Your self-awareness, new insights, and hard work will soon bear fruit or cake, if you prefer. In the next chapter, you'll get equipped with more tools to help you prepare to co-create a relationship vision with your partner. But first, here's a fun and creative exercise to do.

The Circle Game

This exercise gives you a snapshot of how you see your relationship today. People love this exercise and especially enjoy the opportunity for creativity. Consider doing it with friends. People discover all kinds of possibilities. They draw all of their past relationships and compare results. The process stimulates new ways of thinking and elicits surprising insights. It can also be hilarious. Here we go!

Step 1: Start with a blank sheet of paper and colored pencils or fine-line markers. Draw a circle and label it "Me." Inside this circle, jot your unique traits, talents, hobbies, career, and interests. Feel free to jam in as many as will fit. If you need a jump-start, check out the examples on the next page. Just remember: There's no "right" way to do this exercise. A blind approach might be fresh and fruitful.

JERRY'S "ME" CIRCLE

MEG'S "ME" CIRCLE

Step 2: Understand that when two circles (people) form a relationship, a portion of each of their circles overlaps and becomes the "Us." The amount of overlap should reflect the ways in which your lives are joined. You'll get a clearer picture as you read on.

Step 3: Next, draw a second circle labeled "You" to represent your partner. But before you actually draw it, decide how much of your circle overlaps with your partner's (the "Us" space). In some, the amount of "Us" space is a small proportion of the amount of the "You" space in the circle. In others the "Us" space will consume a larger proportion of the space, leaving little room for the "Me" space. Other couples might have circles that don't intersect at all. The variations are endless.

"YOU," "ME," AND "US" — JERRY AND MEG'S CIRCLES

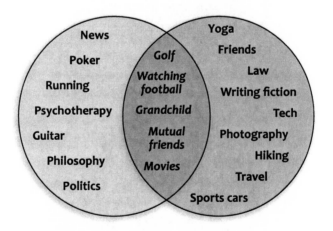

Do you remember Julie and Jim and Chuck and Lisa from chapter 8? Here are their circles:

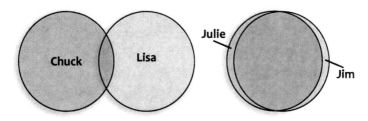

Review and Reflection: What Do Your Circles Mean?

◙ Do the circles differ in size? Which is bigger?

◙ How large is the "Us" space? Does the "Us" space take up the same amount of space in the "Me" and "You" spaces of each circle, or an unequal amount of space?

◙ How much "Me" space is inside the "Us" space? How much is outside of it?

◙ How much of yourself do you give to the relationship?

◙ How close does your depiction come to your ideal relationship? Not enough "Us" space (too distant)? Too much "Us" space (suffocated)?

◙ Are you comfortable with this visual depiction of your relationship?

◙ If you were to make changes, what would your new diagram look like?

◙ Did you draw circles of any of your past relationships? What did they tell you?

All relationships are different. The degree to which your life overlaps with your partner's is a matter of preference and choice. What's important is that you and your partner are comfortable with the structure of your relationship—that you have space enough to feel free and connection enough to feel secure and loved.

Chapter 11

Sharing and Negotiating Your Relationship Vision with Your Partner

Lucy and Roy —
A Controlling Partner Learns to Let Go

Lucy and Roy were referred to me for counseling by their divorce attorney, who suggested they try to save their marriage. Lucy had initiated the divorce, but in the initial meeting, Roy, fifteen years her senior, did most of the talking.

He said, "Lucy, is mixed up, Doc. She doesn't know her own mind, what she wants from life. I think she's depressed. Maybe you can prescribe medication. I think pills would help a lot more than divorce. She won't be any happier without me."

"Lucy, what is your response to what your husband said?"

"I don't know," Lucy replied. It was obvious that if any progress were to be made, I would need to talk separately with each of them. I asked Roy to leave the room.

Lucy was a twenty-nine-year-old who looked about fifteen. When she met Roy four years earlier, her experience with relationships was limited. Lucy felt flattered by the attention Roy showered on her when he ate at the restaurant where she worked as a waitress. She said, "I didn't really have anything going on in my life. I had few friends and no boyfriend. Roy was older, but he seemed nice enough.

"At first everything was okay, but then I couldn't stand his bossiness. He tells me how to do every little thing from loading the dishwasher to styling my hair. He watches everything I do and makes me do it his way. I have no say in anything, even personal matters.

"When I've tried to talk to him he gets angry, very quickly. He can be scary. I mean, he's never hit me, or anything like that, but he is intimidating. I don't think he knows he's a bully, at least with me. I don't really want a divorce, but I can't take it anymore."

Roy, a big man whose hair was thinning at the top, settled into the chair next to my desk. "I don't know what she told you, but this hasn't been easy for me either. When we got married, Lucy didn't know much. She didn't know how to cook, clean, or balance a checkbook. She gets mad when I try to teach her things. Then she pouts. She didn't know the first thing about sex. Now she won't have anything to do with me. Believe me, life with Lucy is no picnic."

Lucy and Roy's inner relationship fingerprints were widely divergent. They expected different things from marriage. They lacked the ability to communicate about their needs and wants, so each of them felt alienated, misunderstood, and alone.

Adopting the Right Mindset — Prepare to Share Your Relationship Vision

In part 1, you explored self-focus and your own wants and needs in relationship. Part 2 is about you *and* your relationship. Soon it will be time to talk to your partner. Before you do, you'll need to equip yourself with the tools to prepare your mental state and pinpoint strategies for effective sharing and persuasion.

Your mindset is the single most important factor to maximize your chance for success. Here are some tips for preparing yourself mentally:

◉ Expect a positive outcome.

◉ Make a list of your needs and wants.

◉ Come to the process with a sense of love and integrity.

◉ Be clear in your own mind what you hope to accomplish.

◉ Be respectful.

◉ Create a positive atmosphere for discussion.

I-Statements Work Miracles

An essential sharing technique to practice and master is the use of *I-statements*. Defensiveness and anger can erupt when one partner blames the other for his or her feelings. Statements that sound like attacks or blaming usually spiral into conflict. Here are some examples:

◉ "You always make me feel guilty."

◉ "You never help in the kitchen."

◉ "You make me so angry."

◉ "You always leave the gas tank on EMPTY."

These word choices sound like accusations and assignments of blame. Statements like these seldom change behavior and are bound to provoke anger and defensiveness.

To avoid these spirals of conflict, you can convert *You-statements* into *I-statements*. For example, instead of saying, "You forgot our anniversary, so you obviously don't care about me," rephrase the statement to say, "I am feeling hurt because you did not remember our anniversary."

With the first statement, the degree to which your partner cares ("You don't care about me.") is a matter of debate. The I-statement is incontrovertible: *Your feelings were hurt.* No one can deny you your feelings.

Let's get the hang of this by reviewing additional examples.

You-Statements	I-Statements
You drive too fast.	*I get scared when you drive at this speed.*
You eat like a pig.	*I worry about your digestion.*
You're always so depressed.	*I see something is bothering you.*
You always leave your clothes around.	*It annoys me to pick up after you.*
You're so noisy when I'm on the phone.	*I'm having a hard time hearing what my mother is saying.*
You're a lousy parent.	*I worry about our children.*

You are probably getting the idea, right? I-statements keep the focus on you by expressing what *you* feel. Use these and your communication with your partner will improve. You'll get more positive responses. Start practicing I-statements for a couple of weeks before you share your relationship vision. With practice, I-statements become automatic and part of your everyday mode of communication. The atmosphere in your home will shift and feel sweeter and calmer.

Strategies for Sharing Your Relationship Vision

Now assuming that you're mentally prepared and expert at I-statements, here are a few strategies for sharing your relationship vision:

Time and Place: Choose an appropriate setting for a meaningful talk. Schedule a block of time to devote to the sharing. Let your partner know the topic so that he or she is not taken by surprise. Select a time when you both have enough emotional and physical energy. Find a location where you won't be interrupted or overheard. Remember: Rome wasn't built in a day. This is a process; these discussions may continue over a period of days or weeks.

Clarity: Be prepared with your own list of needs and wants. Express them clearly and concisely. Ask your partner if he or she understands what you're saying. Clarify if necessary. Make sure your partner really gets it. Keep a sharp focus on the issues. Don't attack or try to win. If you need to cover a number of issues, start first with the less complicated ones. Resolving a few easier matters creates a good track record and sets the stage for successful, cooperative problem solving.

Emotional Climate: Be positive, show respect for your partner, and demand the same in return. Pay careful attention to your tone of voice. Get into a calm, peaceful state.

Cultivate the Right Mindset: Come to the process with a sense of love and integrity. Be clear in your mind what you want to accomplish, and expect a positive outcome. Be patient.

Body Language: Maintain good eye contact. Notice your partner's nonverbal communications. Pay attention to your partner's reactions when you're talking. Understand that you are also communicating nonverbally, and consider what your body is conveying.

Lists: Don't give your partner a list of your wants and needs. This is a prescription for a negative outcome. Instead, share everything, reminding your partner that you are co-creating your vision and can resolve differences together if they arise.

Be Present and Persevering: Do not withdraw if you don't get the response you want. Be persistent. Persevere.

What's in it for Your Partner? Tell your partner how he or she will benefit from the relationship changes you propose. Your partner will have more incentive to talk, persevere, and help make the changes you envision.

Listen: Listen carefully to what your partner is saying. Don't interrupt. Ask questions to learn more. Be curious. Don't formulate responses while your partner is talking. Listen intently until he or she is finished.

Be Creative: You want your efforts to bring positive change to your relationship. An open and creative approach yields the best results. Doing this together deepens and reinvigorates your connection.

Walk in Your Partner's Shoes: Imagine yourself in your partner's place. Think about how your partner will feel being asked to make the changes you propose? What will he or she gain? What will he or she have to give up?

Paving the Road to a New Relationship

Let's assume the best: Your discussions, although not always easy, were productive. Your partner fully understood your vision. You've listened, processed, and understood your partner's responses. Where do you go from here?

Negotiating: Keeping the Vision Alive

Negotiation is the process people use to seek mutually agreeable solutions. Most of the time couples use a straightforward approach. They begin a negotiation in which each partner tries to persuade the other of his or her point of view. In general, each partner is convinced of the correctness of his or her perspective. Each believes that the disagreement stems from the inability of the other to recognize all of the elements of his or her position. Once they get their partner to see each element, the partner will be won over. After, all, doesn't logic always prevail? In fact it very rarely does. Emotion often trumps logic when it comes to love and relationships.

For a successful negotiation, each partner needs to come to the table with a clear intention to strengthen and preserve their union. Both need to benefit. The negotiation approach needs to be a "win-win." Partners who bully or are invested in winning hinder creative problem solving and decrease the likelihood of a positive outcome. During the negotiation process, each partner needs to be free to speak openly and fully without interruption or intimidation. Both need the space to offer their ideas, beliefs, and feelings without fear of criticism, judgment, or threat of retribution. Each partner needs to bring to the table a sense of integrity, respect, and the expectation of a positive outcome. Negotiation is for problem solving, not for power grabbing.

When Do I Compromise?

During a negotiation, you may at times hit a roadblock due to legitimate and opposing points of view. Compromise may seem the only path to resolution. Compromise is not necessarily a bad thing or a sign of weakness. Without compromise there would be no society. People wouldn't be able to live together in communities. Few decisions would be reached. So compromise, by all means, but only after you give careful consideration to the following questions:

◙ Does the compromise eliminate or limit one of your needs or wants?

◙ Is the compromise the best and most creative solution to the problem?

◙ Does the compromise move your relationship in a positive direction?

◙ Did your partner participate in the negotiation in good faith and in an honest, sincere manner?

◙ Did you freely enter into the compromise, or did you feel coerced?

◙ Afterward, will you feel good about the changes the compromise created?

Compromise is easier to accept when it comes from you freely rather than from pressure or intimidation. I find for myself that I will often choose to do something I don't want to do if it feels like an act of love rather than an obligation. Conversely, I'm less likely to do it if I feel pressured by someone else. Like most people, I can be generous on my own initiative, but I'm stubborn when backed into a corner.

What to Do When Your Partner Refuses to Engage or Disengages

It is conceivable that your partner is unwilling to join you in the process of renewal. Despite your persuasion, logic, humor, and persistence, your partner may refuse to budge. He or she may feel the status quo is being threatened and be change-averse. Maybe he or she finds your efforts unimportant or a waste of time. Perhaps your partner feels afraid about exploring his or her inner relationship fingerprint. Whatever the reason, remember that you cannot control another person. Repeat: You cannot control another person. So what should you do next?

Keep the focus on you. Continue on your journey of deepening your self-knowledge. Your thoughts, feelings, and behaviors are in flux and will change over time. As you evolve, it's inevitable that your clarity and intentionality will influence your partner in spite of him- herself. The familiar dynamic begins to erode when one partner stops playing his or her part. The changes in your responses (or lack of response) may confuse or throw your partner off balance, and nudge him or her to participate.

Remember: You are in a period of transition. Not all of your wants and needs will be satisfied, neither will big changes occur until your partner signs on, i.e., enjoying a steamy sex life together, a child, a new house, or a six-month visit from your mother. These require full participation from both partners.

So, don't give up. Persevere in enlisting your partner's coop-eration. You may yet win him or her over. Try some of these specific strategies:

◉ Be persistent.

◉ Don't abandon your needs and wants.

▣ Treasure your relationship vision and spend time thinking about it. Often we attract what we focus on most.

▣ Be persistent.

▣ Try alternative methods of expressing your desire.

▣ Accept that some changes may take longer to manifest.

▣ Be persistent.

▣ Eat some cake.

Crafting Your Relationship Agreement

A relationship agreement supports a co-created relationship vision. The agreement is the culmination of your collaborative effort to reach a specific, desired outcome with your partner through discussion, negotiation, and compromise. The agreement both confirms your present intention and maps out the future direction of your relationship. It's a blueprint of the inner workings of your connection. Be as explicit as possible so as to minimize ambiguity. The clarity and focus of your agreement will help lessen the anxiety that often comes with change.

Guidelines for Writing a Relationship Agreement

▣ Capture the positive intention of your vision.

▣ Maintain respect and integrity for each other.

▣ Detail the responsibilities of each partner.

▣ Include time frames if appropriate.

▣ Determine success metrics if appropriate.

▣ Discuss anxiety and/or fear about performance.

◉ If appropriate, include consequences for not meeting
expectations.

◉ Stay focused — don't get lost in the details.

Regardless of how meticulously you craft your agreement,
unforeseen circumstances may arise. Who knew that you'd win
the lottery or have a new baby on the way? View your agreement as a work in progress that you can revisit. What's most
important is that you and your partner are able to express your
needs and wants and can resolve issues together. Sample agreements are in the appendix and downloadable on our website:
www.freeandconnected.com.

Remember Lucy and Roy, whom we discussed earlier? I met
with them separately for a number of sessions to explore each
of their fingerprints. We paid particular attention to the gaps
between their needs and wants and the reality of their marriage.

Lucy needed more mental, emotional, and physical space — more
freedom. She admitted that she had a lot to learn, but she
wanted to do it on her own terms and in her own time. Lucy
recognized that when she withdrew from Roy, he got angrier
and more controlling, but she didn't know any other way to
get her need for space and autonomy satisfied.

Roy envisioned himself as Lucy's protector and defender.
He perceived her as naïve and innocent, wanted to take care of
her, and show her the ropes so she would benefit from his life
experience. He said, "I'm not trying to be the boss. I'm trying
to help you avoid learning things the hard way like I did."

By the time Lucy and Roy returned for joint sessions, both
had developed clear ideas about their needs and wants in the
relationship. But theirs was a puzzle with very different parts
that didn't easily fit together. Going slowly, each was able to
share with the other his or her vision of their marriage. Lucy
was freedom oriented, while Roy was security minded. Their

ideas about routines, roles, and responsibilities could not have been more different. They had a huge gap to fill.

Lucy and Roy began a series of negotiations that involved working through their inner relationship fingerprints and reshaping the foundation of their marriage. Their perseverance in this complex process was a testament to their love.

Through a unique combination of negotiation and compromise, Lucy and Roy reinvented their relationship. Roy agreed to limit his bossy, paternal behavior. Lucy agreed to assert herself instead of withdrawing. Lucy's renewed commitment to the marriage gave Roy the confidence and incentive to loosen the reins on his controlling behaviors. They began to appreciate their differences as an asset. These changes strengthened their connection and shored up their authentic selves.

What to Do When Negotiation and Compromise Fail

Sometimes a couple just can't agree. If this happens to you, don't despair. Several options are open to move you forward.

Agree to revisit the discussion in three months—a cooling-off period. Given time, partners frequently soften their positions.

Some situations call for a third party. By bringing another perspective, a mediator or therapist can help a couple get unstuck.

Sometimes the gap in a couple's vision cannot be bridged. They may simply agree to disagree, if appropriate. In some situations, the gap makes it impossible to live together and leads to dissolution of the relationship.

The pace of your initial efforts may be slower than you expected. This is all right if no crisis exists and you can cope as a couple. Any progress you've made will motivate you to keep going. Relationship building is a process that requires time, love, and lots of patience. Keep the focus on you. Sharpen your relationship vision. Be intentional in your behavior. Spend time in the still point. Reward yourself with what makes you feel good—a sprig of lilac, a new CD, a candlelit bubble bath, a massage, a DVD of your favorite comedian. Your investment in your relationship is bound to pay dividends. Keep the faith.

Chapter 12

How to Use the Relationship Transformation Methodology to Solve Problems with Your Partner

This chapter demonstrates how to apply the Relationship Transformation approach to solving problems. To illustrate, we selected three typical problem areas that couples face — sex, money, and in-laws. Sex and money problems account for 75 percent of all divorces, and problems with in-laws trail close behind. The following case studies, discussion, and exercises will reinforce the lifelong tools you learned in this book and show you how to use them in dealing with this toxic triumvirate.

Rick and Kathy — A Couple Faces Sex-Drive Disparity

Rick introduced himself. "Our minister referred us to you. We just got back from a weekend retreat sponsored by our church. It was supposed to revitalize our marriage. I'll tell you, Doc, our marriage needs something more like open-heart surgery. That's probably why our minister referred us."

When I asked what was going on, Kathy responded in a quiet voice, "My husband can't keep it in his pants. Rick has slept with at least ten different women—ten that I know about—during our fourteen-year marriage."

Rick responded, "I'm sorry. I feel guilty. I confess my sins, and swear every time I'll never do it again. I remain faithful for a while and our relationship gets better. But then I slip and the cycle starts all over again."

Kathy nods. "I would've left him years ago if it weren't for our three girls. I don't want them to grow up without a father."

"I know there's no excuse for my behavior," Rick said, "but Kathy and I haven't been intimate for a long time, ten years maybe. Really, since our third daughter, Elise, was born. We never had a lot of sex, but after Elise it stopped completely."

They disagreed about the reason their sexual relationship ended. Kathy told me that her sex drive had always been low, and that she had lost interest altogether after Elise was born. Back then, she suspected that Rick was unfaithful, but she felt relieved rather than betrayed.

Rick claimed his unfaithfulness had begun when Kathy shut down their physical intimacy. He declared himself to be a God-fearing man and described his guilt about his infidelities. "Kathy is not the sort of woman who is going to make a scene. We don't have big fights or throw things like some couples. Instead, when Kathy's angry, she goes to the mall and runs up our credit cards—after she's blown through our cash, that is. We're in hock up to our eyeballs."

One of my first goals in treatment with this couple was to stop the cycle of passive-aggressive behaviors. Kathy and Rick were each filled with unexpressed rage. Kathy was angry and hurt that Rick had been unfaithful, but she rarely expressed those sentiments. She shopped to show her displeasure. I believed that by getting her to express her repressed feelings and take responsibility for them, she would stop the excessive shopping.

Rick felt betrayed and angry. He felt that Kathy had also

disregarded her marital vows by refusing to have sex. He didn't want to have sex with Kathy against her wishes. Yet he was driven to satisfy his own sexual desires. He was afraid that if expressed his frustration directly, she would leave him. In the process of therapy, Kathy and Rick developed the skills to directly confront each other with their rage. We will catch up with Rick and Kathy later in this chapter. But first let's wade into the waters of your own sexuality.

Relationships Complicate Sex, and Sex Complicates Relationships

Sex is a complex, multifaceted subject. It is universal to all, yet unique to you. Sex involves biological, psychological, sociological, and anthropological elements. Its meaning changes from culture to culture and generation to generation. Sex is the most basic fact of life, yet it remains a mystery.

If you want nuts-and-bolts techniques, tasty tips, and titillation, this is the wrong book for you. Bookstore shelves and the Internet provide an abundance of that kind of advice. Dr. Ruth, *The Kama Sutra, Cosmo,* and a host of other sources offer more than enough technical advice for a lifetime.

If you want a more fulfilling sex life, you can use the *Relationship Transformation* process outlined in this book and apply it to your sexual relationship.

To begin, remember: keep the focus on you, get into the judgment-free zone, and be kind to yourself. Imagine, even with sex, that it's still all about you. Your sexuality belongs to *you.* Your sexuality is the part of your inner relationship fingerprint that connects to the deepest regions of your being. The expression or inhibition of your sexuality contributes significantly to your self-identity, and influences your personality and how you present yourself to the world.

A sexually repressed person might appear anxious, uncomfortable, and constricted. His voice may be tense, his walk controlled, and his posture caved-in and self-protective. He may convey a kind of timidity. Conversely, a person with full access to his sexuality appears more open, relaxed in his body, and expansive in gesture and language. He may exude confidence and even boldness. Of course, the human psyche and behavior is not always so simple. Some people compensate for their sexual repression by being dramatic, expansive, and outgoing. By contrast, the reclusive librarian might surprise everyone by being a tiger in bed.

Your family, friends, experiences, and culture have influenced the development of your sexuality. Our culture inundates us with mixed messages about sex. The culture is obsessed with the titillation sex provides, but at the same time it enacts laws and encourages prudish and puritanical sexual mores. Throughout history those in authority—secular and religious—have attempted to control the enormously powerful drive that is sexuality.

This cultural ambivalence is confusing. To insulate oneself from exposure to the daily barrage of sexually charged content is impossible. Both pent-up and unrestrained sexuality are responsible for many of the social problems our society faces. The cumulative impact is profound and makes fully owning one's sexuality a challenge. The next exercise focuses on giving you clarity about your sexuality.

Exercise: Your Sexuality

Read and respond to the following statements. Don't overthink. Your first response is usually the most accurate. Keep the focus on you and be kind to yourself. Circle the most appropriate response:

$$T = \text{True}; F = \text{False}, N = \text{Not Sure}.$$

1. I feel sexually satisfied most of the time. **T F N**

2. I would like to have sex more often. **T F N**

3. My partner is a good lover. **T F N**

4. Our sex life is dull. **T F N**

5. My partner is attractive to me. **T F N**

6. I sometimes fantasize about sex with other partners. **T F N**

7. I wish my partner were kinkier. **T F N**

8. Sex feels like an obligation. **T F N**

9. If my partner did certain things, sexual or otherwise, I'd want sex more often. **T F N**

10. I am often too tired to make love. **T F N**

11. I find some things about my partner repulsive. **T F N**

12. After making love, I feel closer to my partner. **T F N**

13. I'll do any sexual thing that my partner asks. **T F N**

14. We often have sex spontaneously. **T F N**

15. I sometimes feel clumsy about sex. **T F N**

16. I usually initiate sex. **T F N**

17. Sex makes me happy. **T F N**

18. I wouldn't care if I never had sex again. **T F N**

19. I worry that my partner is bored sexually. **T F N**

20. Overall, I feel good about my own sexuality. **T F N**

Review and Reflection: Your Sexuality Exercise

Use the following prompts to consider your thoughts and feelings about your sexual self. Write down your responses for future reference.

1. Which, if any, of your responses surprised you?

_____

_____

_____

2. Describe your sexual relationship.

_____

_____

_____

3. What changes, if any, would you like to make in your sexual relationship?

_____

_____

_____

4. Can you talk with your partner about sex in a positive way?

_____

_____

_____

5. How would your partner respond to feedback about your sex life?

_____

_____

_____

Kathy and Rick's Struggle

Remember the struggles of Kathy and Rick, the case study at the beginning of this chapter? Their marriage could not have survived the stress of Rick's affairs and Kathy's refusal to have sexual relations. They needed to break their destructive patterns and create a new dynamic.

In our sessions, both Kathy and Rick were able to express their anger at each other. Over time, by venting their feelings, they were able to let go of old anger and hurt, and move into the present. Rick and Kathy learned to be open about their sexual wants and needs. They knew all too well about the wide gap they faced. Despite feeling discouraged, they persevered. After engaging in intensive dialogue, their anger and hurt gradually receded. With the old baggage lightened, compromise became possible. After a number of stops and starts, Rick and Kathy negotiated and signed an agreement that they both felt good about. They agreed that, for a period of six months, they'd make love one night per week. The specific night would be selected at the beginning of each week. Rick and Kathy felt that while this arrangement lacked spontaneity, their good feelings about rebuilding their relationship more than compensated. At the end of the six months, they would revisit their agreement.

Money Makes the World Go 'Round

What is your relationship with money? Have you ever thought about it that way, as a relationship? It's a complicated topic full of land mines and cultural taboos.

Some people's life purpose is to make and accumulate money. Others try to avoid money, or believe money is evil. Some look down on people who think that money is important. People's connection with money evokes strong emotions: shame, guilt, greed, anxiety, pride, or envy. These emotions often conflict with one another, causing confusion. It is no surprise that money rivals sex as a home wrecker.

You might think of yourself as frugal or generous in your spending patterns. Your economic house could be in good order or total chaos. You might be the kind of person who is comfortable talking about money, or you might find it distasteful. The purpose of this chapter is to help you get a grip on your relationship with money and understand the powerful force it exerts.

Your parents influenced your beliefs, attitudes, and management of money. As a child, you observed their money interactions as a couple and with the outside world. You absorbed your parents' relationship with money without realizing it, in the same way that you internalized your inner relationship fingerprint. In your growing-up years, when you began to have money experiences of your own, you developed your own notions about the value of money. Advertisers, the media, and the culture influenced your notions and those you inherited from your parents. In the rest of this chapter we'll call this bundle of influences and experiences your *money-self.*

The Value of Money

When entering into a love relationship, a person brings his or her money-self along. In the infatuation stage, money is the last thing a couple wants to discuss. If they do, they give it short shrift. Many people think that talking about money is unromantic. A subject fraught with powerful emotional overtones, money hits on our sense of value as a person. In America a person's status is measured by financial net worth rather than by social contribution, academic accomplishment, or artistic genius. Money is equated with happiness.

Advertisers, keenly aware of our vulnerable spots, swoop in

like sophisticated vultures. You've watched the commercials. Advertisers of diamond rings shrewdly manipulate those who equate money with their self-worth. Many men feel inadequate when they buy a small but affordable diamond for their partner. Some women equate the number of carats with the depth of a man's love. Parents feel guilty when they can't afford an I-Phone, I-Pad, the latest computer games, or high-tech sneakers for their kids. How often have you heard politicians blame the poor for their financial condition and talk about them with scorn?

In many circles money is king. Our relationship with money is susceptible to the winds of powerful conflicting emotions. To reconcile our money-self with our partner's money-self is a delicate and complex endeavor.

Exercise: Uncovering Your Money-Self

Are you ready to explore your money-self? Remember the potential land mines, and be sure to keep in mind the usual guidelines: Keep the focus on you. Get into your judgment-free zone. Be kind to yourself. Simply observe your thoughts and feelings. Sorting through the money morass takes time, but it's time well spent. Be honest, but not critical of yourself. No answer is right or wrong. For better or worse, we each have our own unique money-self.

Mark each response True or False. Try to be spontaneous and not over-think your answer. Usually, your first response is the most accurate.

1. I frequently worry about money. T F

2. I never feel that I have enough money. T F

3. If I had more money, I would be happier. T F

4. Money plays a role in many of my decisions. **T F**

5. My partner and I often struggle over money. **T F**

6. Financial problems are a major stress in our relationship.
T F

7. I am a good money manager. **T F**

8. My partner's spending is a problem. **T F**

9. My partner is upset with me about my spending. **T F**

10. I need to control the finances in a relationship. **T F**

11. My family always had enough money. **T F**

12. I struggle to avoid spending. **T F**

13. I need to be in control of my own money. **T F**

14. I get angry watching my partner spend on him- herself.
T F

15. I consider myself frugal. **T F**

16. I stop myself from buying what I want. **T F**

17. I think my partner is a good money manager. **T F**

18. Money is not important to me. **T F**

19. My financial situation makes me insecure. **T F**

20. Money seems to slip through my fingers. **T F**

Review and Reflection:
Gaining Clarity about Your Money-Self

These questions are intended to guide you through the process of discovering your money-self. Getting a handle on how you view money and shining a light on your own inner conflicts is crucial. Clarity about your money-self will lead to more productive conversations with your partner.

1. Did you learn anything about your inner money life?

_____

_____

_____

2. Were there areas of inner conflict?

_____

_____

_____

3. Did you learn anything that you were reluctant to admit, even to yourself?

_____

_____

_____

4. Is money less or more important to you than you thought?

_____

5. Are finances a strain in your relationship?

_____

_____

6. What are your financial needs and wants? Be honest and realistic.

_____

_____

_____

Wrestling with Your Money-Self in Relationships

Now that you've explored your money-self and have a better idea of your relationship with money, it's time to consider how your partner's beliefs, feelings, and practices coincide with or differ from yours. Who's the spender and who's the saver? Is one of you driven to make mountains of money while the other sits in judgment, believing money is evil? Are you more or less generous than your partner about helping others financially or giving to charity? Is one of you satisfied with less? Does one of you want the best of everything? Is your partner too frugal for you? What is the place of money in your life together (i.e., central, scary, stressful, dishonest, peaceful, live and let live, mistrustful, etc.)?

As you already realize, you need to know your money-self to resolve money problems in your relationship. So does your partner (suggest he or she go through the money exercise). If you're both satisfied with your progress, you can move ahead to the next section together.

The Relationship Transformation Process — Resolve Your Money Problems in 6 Steps

Step 1: Focus on you. Use the WYOU and Still-Point techniques in part 1 to tune in to and observe your money-self. Write down what you discover along the way. Take whatever time you need to fully explore your relationship with money.

Step 2: List your specific needs and wants about money and financial security.

Step 3: Make a list of possible outcomes and consequences of your needs and wants, both positive and negative.

Step 4: Share the information from steps 2 and 3. Next, when each of you feels you understand the other's money-self, you're ready to co-create a money vision together.

Step 5: Acknowledge the gaps. Negotiate your options. Compromise, if necessary or if possible. Write a statement of your money vision together.

Step 6: Write an agreement that expresses and supports your money vision.

A Suggestion to Quick-Start the Change Process

Sometimes a money problem can be resolved by a simple fix. Here's a shortcut approach to experiment with. Identify the way finances are handled in your relationship, and then consider whether your current way is the best for you. When intentionally selecting a method, give some thought to what you've learned about your freedom-security styles and inner relationship fingerprint. They bring much to bear on which method might be a suitable match. Here are three options to discuss:

Shared Finances: Couples pool their funds in a joint bank account with equal access for each partner. This is the most common arrangement, especially for couples with children or a single breadwinner.

Separate Finances: Each partner maintains separate accounts and manages his or her own funds. Partners decide the amount of contribution for each toward shared expenses. If one partner earns more than the other, he or she may contribute more than the other. For example, to account for the disparity in incomes, one partner pays the mortgage and the other pays for the food and utilities.

Mixed Finances: Each partner maintains separate accounts and manages his or her own finances. A joint account is created to pay bills. Each partner is responsible to deposit a fixed amount into the joint account to cover his or her share of household and other expenses. Each partner's share can be the same or proportionate to income.

Money Talks

Having a series of adult discussions about your finances goes a long way to diffuse tension. These talks can be uncomfortable and emotionally heated, depending on a couple's financial condition, power imbalances, freedom-security needs, and the impact of the interaction between their individual money-selves. Let the *Relationship Transformation* process for money problems guide you to a positive outcome.

Transform Your Relationship with Your In-Laws

My Aunt Eve used to say, "When you marry a wife, you marry her family." From all that I've observed over the years, she was right. A relationship is an alliance between two families. Each has its own history, beliefs, and customs, and comes with a unique cast of characters with colorful personalities, opinions, and agendas. Each family has its strong points and shortcomings. Some are open to inviting new members into the clan; others are closed systems, judgmental and resistant to anyone new.

Fortunately (or unfortunately, depending on your perspective), most people's involvement with their family continues throughout their life. Some families are close-knit while others are distant. For many people, the process of separating from their family to gain autonomy is long and painful. Often, just as a person has established independent status, he or she settles into a significant relationship that demands cultivating a connection with his or her partner's family. Sometimes it goes well. Other times it can be a daunting obligation.

Michael and Lila

Michael and Lila had been struggling before their first session. As we began, they avoided eye contact with one another. Their anger was palpable. Naturally, I asked them to tell me what was going on.

Michael explained the issue they wanted to address involved his family. His parents had emigrated from Turkey, and although they were secular and westernized, they retained many traditional customs. One of these required all six children and their families to come for dinner at the parents' home every Sunday—no excuses accepted. Each week, twenty-five family members were seated at the table.

Michael continued, "Lila doesn't want to be obligated to go to the weekly dinners. She barely talks, and then usually excuses herself to take a nap. My family thinks she doesn't like them, that she feels she's too good for them."

Lila moved to the edge of her chair. "Heavens, no. I don't think that. I mean, for God's sake, both of Michael's parents teach at Harvard, and are published and distinguished in their fields. I certainly don't feel that I'm better. It's just that I don't want to spend every Sunday with them. I mean *every* Sunday! It takes the whole day. There are other things I want to do with my Sundays. I work all week, clean the house on Saturday, and spend Sunday with my in-laws. What kind of life is that?"

"When we got engaged, you told me you loved my family. Now you don't want to see them? I feel hurt."

"I don't mind seeing them, just not every week."

"Why do you act so remote when you're there?"

"Michael, you might not understand this, but it's not easy for me to connect with your mother and sisters. We're different. I know you disagree, but I'm doing the best I can. You need to let me do this in my own way."

After a cooling-off period of a couple of weeks, Michael and Lila agreed that Lila would go to the Sunday dinner every other week. Michael also agreed to accept Lila's interactions with his family on her terms.

What's the Nature of Your Relationship with Your In-Laws?

If you're like most people, when you met your partner's family for the first time, you wanted to be well received. Everyone wants to be liked, especially in this situation. At the time you might have recognized that each family has its own initiation patterns, which means that the outcome has little to do with you. If the family tended to be rejecting and disapproving, it might not matter how wonderful you actually were. On the other hand, if your partner's family was affirming and supportive, you were likely welcomed into the fold. In most cases, your relationship with your in-laws has its ups and downs and can be challenging at times.

The quiz in the next section will stimulate your thinking and deepen your awareness about the nature of your relationship with your in-laws.

Exercise: Family/In-law Quiz

Instructions: Circle "T" (True) for the statements with which you agree, "F" (False) when you disagree, or "N" (Neutral) if you're unsure or if the statement is sometimes true and sometimes false.

1. My partner's relationship with his family interferes in our life. **T F N**

2. I get along well with everyone in my partner's family. **T F N**

3. I have had arguments with members of my partner's family. **T F N**

4. I like my partner's family. **T F N**

5. I don't feel respected by members of my partner's family. **T F N**

6. I wish my partner stood up to his family. **T F N**

7. My partner's family makes me feel like I belong. **T F N**

8. I enjoy the time I spend with my partner's family. **T F N**

9. My relationship with my partner's family is confusing. **T F N**

10. Members of my partner's family have been rude to me. **T F N**

11. Time is improving these relationships. **T F N**

12. I am closer to my partner's family than my own. **T F N**

13. My values and beliefs are different from my in-laws'. **T F N**

14. My in-laws are sometimes hypercritical. **T F N**

15. I enjoy the closeness with my in-laws. **T F N**

16. I like watching my partner with his or her family. **T F N**

17. I respect my partner's parents. **T F N**

18. My partner's family treats me well. **T F N**

19. I feel no ill will toward my partner's family. **T F N**

20. I am sometimes jealous of my partner's family. **T F N**

Review and Reflection:
Your Relationship with Your In-Laws

The quality of your relationship with your in-laws is bound to affect the quality of your connection with your partner. In-laws are a fact of life. Your relationship with them is a delicate subject worthy of exploration. Consider the following factors to determine the kind of connection you want with them.

- ◙ Your own needs and wants

- ◙ The degree of closeness between your partner and his family;

- ◙ Positive and negative experiences with your in-laws;

- ◙ Geographical proximity to your in-laws;

- ◙ Your desire for children to have a relationship with grandparents;

- ◙ Your ability to set consistent boundaries;

- ◙ Your in-laws' willingness to respect boundaries;

- ◙ Mutual respect.

Finding the Balance

Okay, you're getting close to the finish line. In this last section, you'll evaluate how satisfied you are in your relationship with your in-laws and consider options for change. You might recognize the support and resources they offer as well as the demands they make. It can be tricky to find equilibrium with the many needs, wants, and pressures that compete for satisfaction. Think about your partner's need to maintain a positive connection with his or her family. Appreciate how difficult it can be sometimes for your partner to please you and his or her family at the same time. While completing this exercise, remember to keep the focus on you, stay in the judgment-free zone, and be kind to yourself. Write your responses to the questions below, and set them aside for future use.

Evaluation and Reflection:
Your Relationship with Your In-Laws

How would you characterize your relationship with your partner's family?

_____

_____

_____

Are there changes you would like to make?

_____

_____

_____

Can you talk to your partner constructively about his or her family?

_____

_____

_____

Do you need to change/create any boundaries?

_____

_____

_____

Is your partner's family disrupting your relationship?

_____

_____

_____

What benefits do your in-laws offer?

_____

_____

_____

In-laws can provide certain goodies: love, support, and financial resources that can enhance your life. On the other hand, in-laws can create turmoil and cause anxiety and stress that can erode your relationship if not handled honestly and effectively.

By being clear about your own needs and wants, you can create a relationship with your in-laws that works for both you and your partner. Who knows — there may be yet undiscovered gems. Maybe cake. Let's hope.

Epilogue

Out beyond ideas of wrongdoing
and right doing there is a field.
I'll meet you there.
When the soul lies down in that grass
the world is too full to talk about.

— Rumi

Like Michelangelo's *David,* your beautiful relationship is emerging and slowly beginning to take shape. Guided by your deepest self, you discovered your inner relationship fingerprint. You carefully pared away old beliefs, outmoded roles, and heavy emotional baggage. You released your authentic self and exposed it to the sunlight. You coaxed your partner into the sunny field, and together you envisioned the form of your sculpture. Next you carved, polished, and unveiled this co-creation of your relationship. Take the time to pat each other on the back for your hard work. Celebrate and admire your creation, and feel the excitement, love, and pride in your accomplishment. Eat some cake. Your relationship is transforming before your eyes!

Writing *Relationship Transformation* was a labor of love. It serves as the operating manual in my relationship with my wife, and in my work with clients. I hope the book becomes your guide too.

As you make even the smallest change, your life will transform in unexpected ways. Initiating change takes considerable effort, consistency, persistence, and endless patience. Usually, it takes ninety days to change behaviors and patterns in a lasting way. During this time of transition, remember to stay focused on you and be intentional about your thoughts, words, and actions. Deepen your relationship with your inner life. Be guided by your compelling relationship vision. Keep your eye on the prize—a satisfying, robust love relationship that lasts a lifetime. Here's to your revitalized union—one that gives you space enough to feel free and connection enough to feel safe and loved. You *can* have your cake and eat it too.

Let's continue on our journey together. Stay in touch. Visit us on Facebook or at www.freeandconnected.com.

Jerry Duberstein and Mary Ellen Goggin
2012

Appendix

Scoring for the
Which is Your Attachment Style? Quiz

To score, divide a piece of paper into three sections. Then label each section with one of the three styles: *Secure, Avoidant, and Anxious/Ambivalent.* For each of your answers, give yourself one point in the appropriate section.

1. a. Give yourself 1 point in the "Secure" column if you agreed with the statements in the following questions:1, 2, 3, 5, 6, 8, 9, 17, 20, 21, 23.

   b. Give yourself 1 point in the "Secure" column if you disagreed with the statements in the following questions: 4, 7, 10, 11, 12, 13, 14, 15, 22, 24, 25, 26, 27, 28, 29, 30.

2. a. Give yourself 1 point in the "Avoidant" column if you agreed with the statements in the following questions: 4, 7, 10, 11, 13, 14, 15, 18, 26,

   b. Give yourself 1 point in the "Avoidant" column if you disagreed with the statements in the following questions:1, 2, 5, 6, 8, 17, 20, 21, 23.

3. a. Give yourself 1 point in the "Anxious/Ambivalent" column if you agreed with the statements in the following questions: 12, 16, 19, 22, 24, 25, 27, 28, 29, 30.

b. Give yourself 1 point in the "Anxious/Ambivalent" column if you disagreed with the statements in the following questions: 3, 9.

Tally up the number of points in each column. Your predominant Attachment Style is the one with the highest number of points. If your score is close in more than one Attachment Style, then your style is a blend of the two styles.

Sample Relationship Agreement

The purpose of this agreement is to support our relationship vision. It is intended to encourage communication and to bring clarity to our expectations of each other. It is intended to further ensure our commitment and to encourage our relationship to thrive.

1. Respect

_____

_____

_____

2. Home responsibilities and roles

_____

_____

_____

3. Finance

_____

_____

4. Promises

_____

_____

_____

5. Work

_____

_____

_____

6. Social Life

_____

_____

_____

7. Conflict Resolution

_____

_____

_____

8. Family

_____

_____

_____

9. Concerns and Fears

_____

_____

_____

10. Consequences

_____

_____

_____

11. Duration

_____

_____

_____

12. Modifications

_____

_____

_____

Signed _____

Date _____

Signed _____

Date _____

Sample Relationship Agreement
(Bella and Ed)

In the spirit of their desire to support their Relationship Vision, Bella and Ed agree as follows:

1. Respect – Bella and Ed agree to respect each other as unique adult persons.

2. Home Responsibilities and Roles – Ed will take over the food shopping and cook dinner three nights a week. He will also share equally in all domestic chores.

3. Finances – Bella and Ed agree to change the structure of their financial management. Each of them will open an individual checking account. Each will deposit $2,000 per month into their existing joint checking account to pay household expenses.

4. Promises – Ed and Bella promise to live by their relationship vision. Bella will relinquish her role as the mother. Ed will no longer play victim. Each agrees to accept reminders from the other if he or she relapses into these roles. They will share their thoughts and feelings about their relationship with one another. Bella agrees to spend more time with Ed.

5. Work – Bella and Ed agree to continue to work full-time.

6. Sociability – Bella and Ed agree to respect their differences with regard to their desire for social interaction with others. Ed agrees to offer no mixed messages or resistance to Bella's socializing with her friends and family.

7. Conflict Resolution – Ed and Bella agree to apply the *Relationship Transformation* process to resolve conflicts.

8. Family – Bella and Ed plan to start a family in two years. They agree to share time together with their respective families.

9. Concerns and Fears – Bella is concerned that Ed will regress to needy behavior. Ed fears that Bella will not be sufficiently available to him.

10. Consequences – Ed and Bella agree that if either of them fails to abide by any term of this agreement, they will return to couples therapy.

11. Duration – This agreement will be effective for six months and revisited each month as a reminder of the mutual promises.

12. Modifications: Ed and Bella may modify this agreement, in writing, at any time.

Signed _____

Date _____

Signed _____

Date _____

About the Authors

Dr. Jerry Duberstein has counseled individuals and couples for forty years. He received his PhD in Psychology at Saybrook Institute in San Francisco in 1986 and a master's degree in Counseling Psychology at Antioch New England University in 1976. He lives with his wife, Mary Ellen Goggin, in northern California, where together they lead transformational marriage and couples retreats.

Mary Ellen Goggin has worked with individuals and businesses for thirty-five years as a lawyer, mediator, life coach, and educator. She received her JD at the University of New Hampshire School of Law and a master's degree at Harvard University. Ms. Goggin lives with her husband, Jerry Duberstein, in northern California.

Follow the authors on Twitter @freeandconnected and www.facebook.com/freeandconnected. For additional resources and products go to the website: www.freeandconnected.com.

CPSIA information can be obtained at www.ICGtesting.com
Printed in the USA
BVOW07s1809071113

335729BV00001B/9/P